~ Step Into The Sunshine ~

by LaDonna Wray Thomas

Step Into The Sunshine
by LaDonna Wray Thomas

Printed in the United States of America

ISBN 9781613791110

Unless otherwise indicated, Bible quotations are taken from The New American Standard Bible. Copyright © 1960, 1962, 1963, 1968, 1971, 1972, 1973, 1975, 1977, 1995 by Lockman Foundation.

www.xulonpress.com

"You are light in the Lord. Walk as children of light."
Eph. 5:8

Blessings to you ~
Love ~
LaDonna

Acknowledgements

I want to thank God for never removing the desire to publish this book for Him.

Thank you to my husband, Doug, for his love and patience throughout this procedure. Thank you for respecting my determination to complete the book that began so many years ago.

Thank you to my children, Christina and Chad, and their spouses, Chris and Tracey, for permission to share their lives throughout this book. Thank you for the freedom to be candid and for your encouragement over the years.

Love and many thanks to my mother, Marita. Thank you for your support and encouragement and always being there for your children. I love, honor and respect you.

A special thanks to my clients, many of whom never lived to see this book published. Thank you for your prayers, patience and encouragement as you have shared many of the events in this book.

Thank you to Sue Norton. You encouraged me in the earliest days of this journey. I have never forgotten the time and respect you gave me as you reviewed my earliest manuscript, making many helpful suggestions.

A sincere thank you to Claudia Pfennig for the copious hours you spent transferring my original manuscript from a notebook to a disk. Thank you for your suggestions as well as your encouragement over the years.

Many thanks to Shirley Silver, Sue Edstrom, and D. Ann Burke. I appreciate the time each of you invested proofreading my final submission as well as the encouragement you gave me as I was approaching the *finish line*.

My kindergarten teacher, Mrs. Sarah Lundstrom, in Spirit Lake, Iowa, wrote the following poem in my autograph book when I was five years old. I have never forgotten her words as I skipped all the way home, singing them to myself. When the time drew near for me to begin serious work on this book, I knew her words needed to be included as they will continue to impact my life forever.

"Be a ray of sunshine everywhere you go...shining for your Master with a steady glow."

Table of Contents

Introduction

Nature bursts with illustrations about life. It surrounds us with God's wisdom and purpose, possessing a balance we struggle to obtain. As we observe objectively God's creation and consider the rhythm of the seasons and cycles of our surroundings, it enables us to better understand the Creator of the universe.

In the summer of 1987, while vacationing in McCall, Idaho, I became sharply aware of the natural beauty surrounding me and began to see people and situations demonstrated by God's handiwork.

My husband, Doug, and our son, Chad, were fishing at one of the crystal clear lakes that snuggle into the majestic mountain ranges, beautifully framing the restful hamlet of McCall.

I don't have a love for fishing, but I do enjoy traipsing along for the scenery and exercise. Our daughter, Christina, and I discovered the perfect observation point, spreading our blanket on top of a huge rock that jutted out into the lake. The sun was shining brightly, causing the water to glisten and dance beneath the most awesome blue sky I had ever seen. The rock was warm as we stretched out to supervise, but a chill hung in the air as snow still covered several of the peaks surrounding the lake.

Not far from us was a towering pine tree that stood as tall and straight as a rocket on its launching pad. Next to the base of this gigantic tree was what appeared to be a perfect little pine tree. I pointed this tree out to Christina, and she was impressed with how perfect it appeared. We agreed it would be a perfect Christmas tree. I suggested she walk closer to investigate the backside, which was hidden from our view.

She was disappointed because the tree she had envisioned as being so perfect had no branches on its backside. I said, "Christina, I hope you never marry a man like that big tree!" We both laughed and began to relate to these trees. Everywhere we looked, we could see familiar people and situations illustrated in nature.

The rock we were resting on was eight to ten feet thick. Through a crack in this rock grew two wild flowers. We were amazed at the persistence and perseverance of these two fragile flowers. Those flowers represented our dear friends, George and Martie Hage. Martie had been battling lung cancer for three years. Through all the discouraging setbacks the couple continued to grow stronger in their faith and "bloom" through the hardest of times.

Martie lost a battle with cancer but won the prize that was promised to her in God's Word. (Phil. 3:14). She was faithful to the point of death and received the crown of Eternal Life. She now dances on "the streets that are golden" in the presence of her precious Lord and Savior, Jesus Christ.

I have known women married to men who dominate their lives, or who have been so intimidated by situations in their past, that their lives are much like the underdeveloped pine tree. For example, women in abusive marriages who have taken the situations they experienced in their lives as their identity. They will never see themselves as God sees them and will not experience the potential God had intended for their lives.

Childhood trauma, physical, emotional, sexual, alcohol and substance abuse have also robbed many women and men from discovering their special gifts and talents. So often we are not even aware that we have been deprived of the precious element that causes us to grow.

The sun is the life blood of growth for almost every species of plants or foliage. Flowers depend on the sun for prolific blooms and foliage for its rich color mass. Without the sunshine our physical and emotional health suffers as well. Webster's Dictionary describes "sunshine" as a source of "cheer and happiness."

It wasn't until later when I pondered the revelation of our day in the woods that I realized I was "that little pine tree." My husband Doug is not at all like the one I suggested the larger tree represented and cautioned Christina never to marry. He has never dominated me or cast a shadow on anything I set out to accomplish. Doug is quite the opposite. He has been supportive, and once he understands my plan and catches my vision, he can be very encouraging.

However, I was standing in the shade of my husband and children and part of my life was underdeveloped, lacking depth and direction...much like the spindly branches on the backside of the tree that had caught our attention and created our conversation.

I was known as Doug's wife or Christina's and Chad's mom. Each of these identities I cherished. However, like that little pine tree, I wasn't catching enough "sunshine" to fully develop into the woman God intended me to become.

I felt enlightened by this revelation, and excited to share what I had discovered. I began to think of interests that I had never pursued. I always had a desire to paint or express myself artistically. I enjoy decorating, which includes upholstering furniture and accessories to create an inviting and restful environment in our home. I realized that God offered me 'gifts' that I had never opened. By not opening these 'gifts,' I would not only deny myself the pleasure of exploring them, but would also not contribute them to my children's inheritance.

I realized it was time to "expose my backside" to the sunshine and allow growth to take place.

Children need to see gifts demonstrated to recognize talents they may possess. For instance, if you have had an admiration for artwork, sign up for a community education class and try your hand at it. You may be surprised at the talents that lie beneath the surface. This could be a talent that your children may possess as well.

Consider creative cooking, sewing, needlework, gardening, decorating and yes, even writing. Your children will benefit from the larger fields that you explore, being more likely to express their interests because of your example. However, their interests may be very different from yours, which will add an even larger list of gifts from which your grandchildren and others will benefit.

Over the years several family members and friends have received letters from me that, if numbering pages, could be classified as books. I never saw myself as writing an actual book, but when we returned home from McCall I felt so encouraged and enlightened that I began to scribble thoughts on pieces of paper and even napkins, tucking them away as little treasures.

As I began to meditate about our time in the woods, thoughts continued to permeate my thinking and the words "Step Into The Sunshine" flooded my mind. I immediately knew this was to be the title of my book. I combed the aisles of several bookstores, making sure the title had not been taken. I knew this book was not something that would be completed quickly. We still had several years of raising Christina and Chad as well as learning what the Lord would show me through the process.

I tucked notes in every imaginable place when thoughts and illustrations would flood my mind. Doug bought me a small tape recorder, since I would often be inspired with some of the best ideas while driving to or from work. I'm sure he helped me avoid several rear-end collisions as I would scribble thoughts on post-it tablets attached to my steering wheel while waiting at stoplights. I began taping my ideas while ironing, and would jot notes on prayer request cards while sitting in church. Eventually I put recipe cards in my Bible so I would have note material available.

Here I am, at least five years later, (1992) back in McCall. This time by myself, starting this labor of love, "Step Into The Sunshine." Won't you join me as I am discovering every day that there is joy in the journey as we learn to step into the sunshine and grow in God's grace?

Allow the Lord to open your mind and heart to the areas in your life that may be underdeveloped and in need of a little 'sunshine.' As you read about my life journey, I pray that it will help you to relate to your own journey. I know the Lord will point out to you the shaded areas in your life that are in need of attention, exploration and sunlight.

God is gracious and patient as he encourages us to move beyond the place perhaps others have planted us or we have refused to move from over the years. Get ready for the Creator of the universe to gently guide you beyond your wildest dreams or expectation. He will prune, pamper and protect you from your greatest fears as He positions you for His purpose, as only He can do.

"We have one life, 'twill soon be past, only what's
done for Christ shall last."

The following is a prayer I wrote in a journal the day I began work on this book.

June 23, 1992

Dear Lord,

I know You have plans for my life. I also realize my life so far has been a part of that plan. I pray that I will know Your plan, that I will seek Your direction, and that I will do Your will. You have blessed me with so much that I pray one day I may give back something special to You, through the lives of others You've allowed me to touch, hearts that are open, and eyes that are ready to see You.

I pray Your blessing upon this book. I have so much I want to share, and I pray You'll bring to my mind all the challenges and situations throughout the years that You would want in this book. Help others to see You and be blessed by You as they read. Help me not to get sidetracked on material that isn't necessary. Also, help me to remember: "when others saw a shepherd boy, God saw a King." Just because I've never considered myself a writer doesn't mean I can't write a book with Your help. I am claiming Philippians 4:13 . . . "I can do all things through Him who strengthens me."

Help me not to grow discouraged, and to look forward to spending time with You daily. May Your Word be my constant source of renewal and inspiration for this book. Thank you Lord, for this desire You've placed in my heart, and for the encouragement from others.

In Jesus name ~ Amen

Chapter 1

Recognizing the Shade

Realizing what was keeping me from the fullness of God's light in my life.

" *Is this from the Lord?... A spirit of death has surrounded LaDonna and has not let the fullness of My Light in,"* were words scribbled on a piece of paper and passed to another woman.

"Did you know her first husband died?" was the woman's response as she handed the piece of paper back to her friend.

This note was handed to me during a break at a Woman's retreat I was attending. The two women who were corresponding through this note were not well acquainted with me at the time. They approached me to see how I would respond to the words that Lydia had received from the Lord. The note that was passed from one woman to another revealed a shade in my life I didn't realize existed.

I married my high school sweetheart when I was eighteen years old. Bill and I had gone steady from the time I was fifteen, and were engaged my senior year. Although Bill was a year older than me, he still had a year of high school to complete. We promised our parents he would finish school if we could get married after I graduated in 1968. With their consent, we were married August 10, 1968.

We had a beautiful wedding with all our family, friends and what seemed to be the entire High School attending. My sister, Linda, was my matron of honor and our close friend, Doug, was Bill's best man. Doug and Bill had been best friends since they were eleven years old.

Keeping our promise, Bill worked nights at the sawmill while attending High School during the day. I worked at the Ranger Station for the U.S. Forest Service. We not only had to keep our word to our parents about

Bill graduating, but to all the teachers at Darby High School as well.

We both loved children and were excited to learn that I was expecting in June of our second year of marriage. If we had a boy we had chosen the name Douglas Neal. Douglas after our best friend, Neal for Norman, Bill's father, Edward, for Bill's grandfather and Laythol, my father. Four months into the pregnancy I miscarried, which left us deeply disappointed.

After losing the baby I remember telling Bill and my mother I didn't feel we would ever have another child. Of course they assured me the doctor found no medical reason for the miscarriage, a second pregnancy would just be a matter of time. Our dreams seemed to be dashed though, and I was heartbroken.

Our disappointment was soon overshadowed by the draft notice Bill received from the US Army. Deciding to take a different course, Bill joined the National Guard and was stationed at Ft. Knox, Kentucky to complete his basic training.

While Bill was in Kentucky we were corresponding about what we would do when he returned home. We began to make plans to go to Denver where my dad lived. Dad said there were many job opportunities for my brothers so we decided to throw caution to the wind and join them. Like most young couples we spent hours making plans for our future. A change of scenery and a new adventure was just what we needed.

Bill contacted his friend Doug asking if he would be interested in joining us for a summer of working in Colorado. My dad had located jobs for my brothers, Duane and Daryl, and said there would be plenty of work for Bill and Doug as well.

I had been living with Bill's parents while he was at Ft. Knox. They were wonderful, treating me more like a daughter than a daughter-in-law. We were all anxious for Bill to return home and for us to resume our life together as a family.

We had an apartment ready to move into when Bill arrived home from his basic training. He was looking forward to seeing our families and friends, sharing his experiences of the last four months in Kentucky as well as our plans of going to Denver.

A week after Bill returned we had a wonderful day with Bill's six-year-old brother, Ray, also known as 'Moose.' Ray had missed his big brother who he followed like a shadow and especially loved riding in our red Mustang. We took Ray for a drive and a picnic in the mountains. We wanted to spend as much time as we could with him, knowing we would be leaving town again soon.

After returning Ray to his parent's home, Bill and I were spending the evening with our friends Pat and Judy. While we were playing cards we received a call inviting us to a going away party for a mutual friend who would be leaving for Vietnam. We didn't especially feel like going, but decided we would for a while, allowing Bill to see some of his buddies and perhaps exchange stories of their military experiences.

When we arrived, the house was packed with people. Everyone was having a great time renewing old friendships and dancing. The music was loud, making it hard to visit. There weren't many seats available, so I sat on Bill's lap. As he was telling a story, he spilled his drink. I left the room to get a cloth to wipe up the spill and when I returned, Bill was gone. I looked around, visiting with people, asking if anyone had seen Bill. No one seemed to know where he had gone. Through the loud music and conversation I could hear a siren. I got a sick feeling in the pit of my stomach – I just knew it was Bill.

"He just went out doors for some fresh air," one of our friends tried to reassure me as I expressed my fears to him. We all ran out of the house to look for our car, but it was nowhere to be seen.

When you hear an ambulance siren in a town the size of Darby, chances are that you will know the person being transported. Within a matter of minutes everyone from the party had jumped into their cars, racing to see who the ambulance was for. With everyone gone, I looked around and the only person I saw was Bonnie. She looked at me and with the same fear in her voice that I was feeling she said, "I saw Albert talking to Bill, but I didn't know they had gone anywhere."

We stood in the front yard clinging to one another not knowing what to do. A car raced down the street and came to a screeching stop in front Bonnie and me. The driver jumped out of the car and said he was looking for Mrs. Lee and Mrs. Sturgis. We quickly climbed into his car as he took us to the scene of the accident. When we arrived there were so many vehicles and people on the highway that we couldn't get close to the ambulance.

I later learned that my brother, Duane and his girl-friend, Carolyn, had gone to a movie with their friend, Dave. Duane was looking for Bill to borrow his car to take Carolyn home after the movie. They had passed Bill and Albert going the opposite direction through town. Before Dave could turn around to catch up with him, they heard a crash as Bill's car flipped end over end several times as he attempted to round the long curve on the edge of town.

Duane, Carolyn and Dave were the first ones on the scene of the accident. They saw the car immediately, but Bill and Albert had both been thrown from the wreckage. The highway department had burned the ditches that day making it difficult to find Bill and Albert in the dark.

When they located Albert, who was severely injured but conscious, he kept saying, "You need to find Bill."

Dave stayed with Albert as Duane and Carolyn quickly began to comb the borrow pit for Bill. When they finally located Bill at the top of the borrow pit, he was not conscious. Carolyn stayed with him while Duane ran for help.

The closest home belonged to the family of the nurse who assisted in the ambulance when called on emergencies. Duane pounded on the door, yelling for help, waking the family. Ann quickly threw on a pair of shoes and ran through the field in her pajamas with Duane after she summoned the ambulance.

By the time I arrived, Duane was there to meet me and told me not to go to our car. Bill and Albert were already in the ambulance, which would be heading for the closest hospital in Hamilton, fifteen miles away. The car Bonnie and I were in followed close behind the ambulance

I can remember thinking how slow the ambulance seemed to be going, and how glad I was I had paid the insurance on the car. Bill only made $80.00 a month while he was in the National Guard. In March he suggested I buy myself something for my birthday.

Something special for when he came home. The car insurance was due the same time. I chose instead to pay the insurance.

When we arrived at the hospital, there were already several people from Darby gathering on the front lawn. Friends from the party, people who had been in the bars downtown and others who had heard the siren and figured, since Darby was such a small town, that it was someone they knew. We watched as the ambulance attendants removed Albert. I could see his bright yellow jacket on the gurney, so I knew it was him. They took much longer removing Bill, which upset me terribly. When they finally removed Bill, we all raced into the hospital.

When we entered the small waiting room, we could hardly make our way through the group of people who were continuing to gather. I asked to see Bill, but the nurses said the doctors were working on him and that, "He was going to be fine." A few minutes later another nurse came through the waiting room and said to me, "He will be fine; you will be able to see him soon."

Through the large window in the waiting room facing the street I saw Bill's parents arrive, running up the steep front steps. How I hated the thought of them learning that Bill was hurt. They loved him so much.

When they made their way through all the people waiting for information, Bill's dad wouldn't hear of staying put. Pushing his way past the nurses, he went immediately into the emergency room. Bill's mother and I stood in shock waiting for his return. A nurse gave Fern something to calm her, since she appeared ready to pass out.

A short time later, Bill's father returned with a dreadfully solemn look on his face. He gathered his wife with one arm and me with the other and held us tight. We both squirmed to get away to see Bill, but his arms remained clenched around us.

I said, "I want to go see Bill. Why won't they let me see him?" He looked at me with eyes filled to the brim and said, "Bill isn't anymore." The words rang in my head like a freight train passing through. I couldn't process what I was hearing.

Bill's mother collapsed into a nearby chair as her eyes rolled back in her head. There was a blur of confusion as the news made its way through the waiting room. Disbelief, tears, shock, anger. Emotions were raw at that moment.

What I did next is something I'm not proud to write. My mother had arrived by this time, and I asked her for my dad's phone number. My parents were divorced and my dad lived in Denver at the time. My dad had an uncanny ability of predicting things. He took great pride in his predictions and it would drive me crazy how his predictions would often be correct.

When Bill and I were married, I was told that my dad had made the comment that our marriage wouldn't last two years. This made me so angry. Bill and I couldn't wait to show him he would be wrong with this prediction.

When I called my dad the first thing I said was, "I wanted to be the first to tell you that you were right again. We didn't last two years. Bill is dead!" I think my mother took the phone from me, filling him in on the details. His wife told me later that he cried when he got off the phone, terribly sorry for having made the comment.

As the news spread throughout the small community, one of our good friends knew he needed to call Bill's best friend Doug, who was attending college in Dillon, Montana, to inform him of Bill's death. Doug was living with his sister, Kenna, and her family at the time. When they received the devastating phone call, Doug's sister and brother-in-law packed their three small children in the car to drive Doug to Darby immediately. As they were getting ready to leave, Doug remembered Bill's sister, Vicki, who was attending college in Dillon as well. He went to the dormitory and gently told Vicki of her brother's accident, inviting her to ride with his family to get her home as soon as possible.

While they were en route to Darby, Doug spotted Bill's dad racing to Dillon to pick up Vicki. Heavy hearts processing the tragedy that impacted so many lives as Vicki transferred into the car with her father.

The next few days were a blur of decisions. Choosing a casket, the clothing Bill would wear, the flowers, insurance details, writing the obituary, as well as arranging the funeral. The four young men who had been Bill's best man and groomsmen just two years earlier were now being called to serve as pallbearers, carrying Bill to his final resting place.

Bill was loved by so many and was the apple of his dad's eye. It nearly broke his grandfather Ed's heart. He adored Bill and had so many hopes for his future. I'll never forget Bill's little brother, Ray. He was trying to be so brave, trying hard not to cry. The brother Ray had waited for so long to come home from basic training, would never come home again.

I remember doing Bill's mother's, grandmother's and aunt's hair the morning of the funeral. I was void of emotion. I'm sure, looking back, that I was in a state of shock. Because I was void of emotion, I was afraid I wouldn't be able to cry at the funeral, and worried about what people would think. I'm not sure why we try to be so brave during the darkest times we experience in our lives. I guess we think we're supposed to, for everyone else. I didn't really have a handle on "living" at the young age of twenty, much less "dying."

Friends were with me constantly. I would go to our apartment to get some rest, and there were always several friends playing cards quietly, never allowing me to be alone. My brother, Duane, was always by my side. He and Carolyn, who is now my sister-in-law, were great comforts. There will always be a special bond as they shared such a painful experience with me.

Bill's funeral was huge...so many people coming to offer love and support to all Bill's family and me. The building was crammed with people as well as several who had to stand on the front lawn of the facility.

I had a heart shaped wreath made for Bill with red, white and blue carnations and a ribbon with "SWEETHEART" on it. I placed the heart on his casket after the final prayer at the cemetery. When I went back by myself hours later, I couldn't find the wreath among the flowers that had been placed on Bill's grave. I later learned that Doug's stepfather, Lyle, who had dug the grave, left the wreath on the casket where I had placed it. That somehow gave me comfort, knowing it was close to Bill.

A couple days after Bill died I was still receiving letters from him, as well as letters addressed to him from friends he had made during basic training. I also received his final paycheck and formal photographs the army had taken of him in his uniform. At the time I couldn't fully realize the confusion I was feeling. There were moments when I imagined the last week was all a bad dream and Bill would be home soon. I seemed to slip from reality to hopeful possibilities as I processed my grief.

Bill's family was in shock. Losing a child has to be one of the most painful experiences any of us could ever have. I had always been close to Bill's family. They had treated me like a daughter from the time Bill and I started dating. His sister, Vicki, and I were cheerleaders together. I stayed in their home while my family was in Iowa the summer before we were married. As lost and confused as I was at the tender age of twenty, they were devastated.

Bill's father had lost not only a son, but a friend. They had been so close. I can remember calling his father to see if I could come to their home to gather some of the remaining belongings I had stored with them. We were both heartbroken. I had made the decision to move to Denver with my dad, as Bill and I had planned earlier. I'm sure Bill's family was disappointed with me for leaving so soon after Bill's death. They probably felt as if they had lost us both.

I made the comment to Bill's father while I was picking up my belongings how we had all lost someone different in our lives. I had lost a husband, he and Fern lost a son, Vicki and Ray lost a brother. I remember saying how painful it was for all of us, and how we couldn't know the pain the others felt.

In his grief and through his pain he said to me, "I hope someday you'll have a son, and he'll be killed and then you'll know how I feel." With those words ringing in my ears I left in tears. I thought time would heal the sting of his hurtful comment and hoped that one day we would speak again.

My three brothers, Duane, Daryl and Dennis, our friend Doug, and I headed for Denver as we had planned before Bill's accident. There was no life for me in Darby. My dad had jobs for all of us in Denver, so we set out for a new experience. None of us had ever been to Colorado, so amid the grief was the anticipation of a new beginning. Having our best friend Doug with us helped as he shared the pain and loss we were all experiencing.

Doug and I had been through so much and shared a great loss. It made sense for all of us, including Doug, to continue with the original plan of moving to Denver to work for the summer.

I never went back to live in the town that harbored so much grief. I carried the hurtful words that were spoken to me for years. Once I realized that those words were keeping me in bondage, I finally forgave Bill's father for what he spoke in the depths of his grief. I never saw him again before he died, which removed my hopes of ever reconciling with him.

Bill and I had attempted to take a second honeymoon on two occasions. Both times, at the last minute, Bill thought it would be fun to asked Doug if he would like to invite a friend and join us. I would end up sharing a room with the girl Doug invited, and Bill and Doug would share a room. I shouldn't have been surprised since we called Doug from Yellowstone Park while we were on our honeymoon to see what everyone was doing. In fact, we came home a day early because there was something going on at home, and we were afraid we'd miss out on the fun. (Did I mention we were young when we got married?) I never minded, because I always enjoyed Doug's company. We were in the same class and were great friends. I was always "one of the guys," going everywhere with Bill and his friends.

Doug and I were coeditors of our newspaper and yearbook, voted Sophomore, Junior and Senior favorites. Our Senior year we were named Mr. and Miss Darby High School. We had so much in common, but the greatest bond was our mutual relationship with Bill.

My three brothers and Doug started work right away and I found a job at a drive thru "Photo Mart." The summer went quickly as we all were busy and helping one another process the loss of a husband, brother-in-law and friend. We returned to Darby for my brothers to start the school year.

Four months after Bill died, I married Doug. My love for him had changed and grown from that of a friend to that of a husband. I knew in my heart that Bill would never want me to be with anyone but Doug. While Bill was in Ft. Knox, he would write to Doug asking him to watch out for me and make sure I wasn't just sitting home while he was gone.

I never had second thoughts once we decided to get married. However, I was concerned about how the news would be received by our families, especially Bill's. I knew it would likely be very hurtful to Bill's family, and that was the last thing I wanted to do. At the same time, I knew without a doubt that I wanted to spend the rest of my life with Doug.

On September 9, 1970, we headed for Salt Lake City after saying, "I do" in Salmon, Idaho and never looked back. We knew we were on our own, and all we had was each other. We didn't know exactly how our friends or families felt. We knew we had made an important decision, and we were prepared to stand behind it. I have never once regretted the decision to marry Doug.

The song, "We've Only Just Begun," by the Carpenters, was playing on the radio. "A kiss for luck and we're on our way," definitely took on new meaning for us as we headed out of town that morning into a future we had never anticipated.

Out of respect for Bill's family we kept our plans to ourselves. We told our families the night before we left, and asked the courthouse to omit our marriage information from their newspaper. No such luck and very naive on our part as it was a matter of public record. It came out in the paper the next day and, small world that it is, someone who once lived in Darby and worked in Salmon, saw the marriage announcement and called his family and friends. The news spread like wildfire.

Looking back from my age and perspective today, I would have been more sensitive to the timing. I realize now my decision to marry so soon after Bill's death created a lot of hurt for Bill's family. I regret any pain I caused them or confusion that our family and friends may have experienced.

When Bill died so suddenly, I became dreadfully aware of how our lives are but a vapor and each day is an opportunity to live that day to the fullest.

After so many changes in such a short period of time, I realize I had never really grieved for Bill. I was so concerned with making sure everyone else was doing okay, that my own emotions were locked away to be dealt with at a later time. That later date never did come. I didn't want Doug to feel like he was a substitute for Bill. I suppressed my grief, not knowing what to do with the pain and confusion that surrounded the night Bill died.

When we left town the day we were married, I thought I could begin a new chapter in my life. Bill's memory would always be safe in both of our hearts, as Doug and I both loved Bill and have never forgotten him. We spoke of Bill often and would recall all the good times we had with him. However, I had never grieved.

Several years later on the day the two women exchanged the note at the Women's Retreat, I believe it was God's timing for me to grieve for the first time. I began to sob as if I was having convulsions. They prayed for me, and I know the Lord was healing a wound that went dreadfully deep. It was like a bright light was shining into my innermost being, exposing years of denial and behaviors that had developed in the "shade."

Just like the little tree that stood at the base of the tall pine tree, I recognized that I stood in the shade of my anger at Bill for having ended his life by driving too fast. I was angry with Bill for leaving me alone at such a young age. I was in the shade of my anger toward my dad for his statement of our marriage not lasting two years. I was in the shade of my anger toward Bill's dad for being so hurtful with his words when he said he hoped I had a son one day and he would be killed so I would know how he felt. I was in the shade of my guilt for having married Doug so soon after Bill died.

When Doug and I got married, I snuggled in close to him. I became part of his life and began to take on his identity. It was a safe place to be as I felt so loved and understood with Doug. I didn't need to explain my feelings to Doug since he shared them as well. I didn't need to explain about what had happened in my life, he knew all the details. I was like a scared, wounded animal that had retreated into a safe, familiar cave. Doug was my security and shelter. I feared processing the grief because I didn't want Doug to confuse the delayed reaction. I shut the door tightly, not thinking I would ever have to enter that time in my life again.

The Lord did not leave me broken by this exposure. He gently moved me to a position of experiencing His love more completely as He patiently waited for me to recognize and release my anger and disappointments to Him. I chose to pick up my roots and step into the sunshine. I needed to take responsibility for my choices.

Are you standing in the shade of someone or something? It could be a job, an addiction, wrong thinking, insecurities from experiences in the past, or it could be a form of abuse. We all have choices. Often our fear prevents us from making choices that will create positive changes in our lives.

Zig Zigler, a highly respected motivational speaker, often says, "People are so busy being angry about the past and fearful of the future that they are paralyzed in the present."

Does this sound familiar? We usually have to conquer anger and fear to accomplish anything substantial. Remember, you don't have to do it alone. The Lord knows your fear and is aware of your anger more than you can imagine. He also knows this duo could rob you of your future.

Jeremiah 29:11-13 says, *"For I know the plans that I have for you, declares the Lord, plans for welfare and not for calamity to give you a future and a hope. Then you will call upon Me and come and pray to Me, and I will listen to you. And you will seek Me and find Me, when you search for Me with all your heart."*

I don't know about you, but I would rather trust my future to the One who created me and has promised that I have a future with Him, than to wander through life not realizing the importance of the sunshine that is available to everyone.

Learning to recognize the shade in our lives helps us to choose to step into the fullness of the Light that causes the darkness to flee.

SHADE: Comparative darkness caused by the screening of rays of light. A place or areas sheltered from light.

Something used to reduce or shut out light. (Webster's Dictionary)

Points to Ponder...

Can you identify a time in your life when you realized you were standing in the shade?

How do you feel the shade affected your growth?

How has it affected your relationship with God?

Chapter 2

Preparing the Soil

How God overturned the soil in my life, preparing it for new crops.

During one of our Women's Ministry meetings, a friend explained that she had listened to a speaker who said God was responsible for the soil. We are responsible for the planting.

I considered this in my own life. I think there have been times when I have wanted to put a little "top soil" in places, when in fact, that is not my responsibility.

The Lord gives us opportunity to plant the seeds and offer water, but I have come to realize that the soil and pruning are His responsibility. He is aware of the condition of the heart, which no one else can know. The heart is where the growth in a person's life takes place.

In preparing an area for a garden, you wouldn't just toss the seeds on the ground or take a sharp stick, poking the hardened soil and drop seeds into the holes. The poor little seeds wouldn't have a chance to germinate and grow.

Preparing the soil is important for the tender roots to be able to reach their full potential. The ground needs to be turned, breaking up clumps of dirt that have hardened from lack of water or from not being used. You would also remove remnants from last year's crop and perhaps might apply fresh top soil, rich in nutrients. A similar phenomenon seems take place in our lives as well. Our soil, or lives, are often overturned, preparing us for what God is purposing to do through each circumstance that we encounter.

Several years ago I asked my friend Debbie, who worked for *Hershey's*, if I could ride along with her as she called on her accounts. I thought it would be relaxing to visit with her, jotting down some thoughts while she would go into the different businesses to restock their candy supplies and take orders. Debbie had a restful route, traveling through several rural towns and picturesque landscapes, scattered with orchards and family farms.

It was in late autumn and the trees and foliage along the road were in full color. Every gentle curve as we meandered through the countryside would give way to breathtaking scenes of clusters of crimsons and golds.

The fields had been put to rest for the winter as the crops had been harvested, leaving miles of barren hillsides. The fields that had recently been lush, green and growing, had now been prepared to rest for the winter. I had never considered the importance of resting the soil.

As we traveled from town to town I began relating to the soil as I desperately needed a time of resting from my daily routines. I needed time in a different environment to be able to observe nature and to gather thoughts for this book God had placed on my heart to write.

After writing notes throughout the day, I realized I was feeling guilty about taking the time to relax and do what seemed to be 'nothing productive' since it was so enjoyable. My notes reflected this notion. As I reread what I had written a few days later, I saw truth in so many of my random thoughts that I had captured. I was convinced that it was not only acceptable but necessary to have days set aside for rest and a break from routine.

In caring for ourselves, we **are** caring for others. If we use up everything within us, we have nothing left to give. Women have a nurturing nature and we typically take care of everyone else before ourselves. We live in a constant state of overdrive. There is always one more thing we need to pick up, or to put back into its proper place.

I have been a hair stylist since 1979 and constantly see women in juggling acts. Driving children to practice, errands to run, groceries to be picked up, having to be back to work within 45 minutes, dry cleaning to drop off, and still not sure what to have for dinner tonight! It is difficult to schedule haircuts, colors and perms within an already over scheduled calendar. My clients look forward to the time in my chair as it is often the only opportunity they have to sit still, relax, and have someone do something for them.

Women who don't work outside the home or aren't married don't have much more free time than those of us who do. It's crazy out there in our fast pace world! There are times we find ourselves living in the eye of the hurricane and don't seem to know how to get out of it gracefully.

"Don't confuse renewing your mind with wasting your time." This thought was one of my notes that caused me to pause and rethink an old mindset. The idea that resting or simply enjoying myself is wasting time was a lie from Satan that I refuse to listen to anymore. I believe one of Satan's deceptions is to keep us so busy that we will not rest at the feet of Jesus.

I am reminded of Mary and Martha in Luke 10:39-42. Mary was drawn to the feet of Jesus, captivated by every word Jesus had to say. This of course irritated her sister, Martha, as she was busy preparing a meal for Jesus and His followers. When Martha complained to Jesus for her sister's lack of help, Jesus assured Martha that Mary had chosen what was necessary. She had chosen to listen to what Jesus had to say.

I can certainly relate to Martha as far as putting the "to do list" first. I often long for peace and quiet without phones, television, or radio. Just complete silence. Even when I do find quiet time, my mind is constantly running. That is why riding along the backcountry roads with my best friend, Debbie, was so relaxing. It was a change of scenery, and I knew I had set aside time to capture random thoughts on paper.

I am happy to report that I now have a split personality. I have learned to sit at the feet of Jesus every morning spending time in His Word as well as reading a variety of devotionals. This time I purpose to set aside each morning fills me with truth, hope and encouragement. It enables me to encourage others and to be better prepared to navigate through whatever events may unfold throughout the day. I have found these two "Mary - Martha" personalities or traits can coexist beautifully. They are both necessary in our homes as well as in our churches.

This is demonstrated by serving God with our *hearts* and our *hands,* which is reflected in Mark 12:30. "And you shall love the Lord your God with all your heart, with all your soul, with all your mind, and with all your strength."

Every spring the fields are plowed, making the soil ready to receive the seeds that the farmer has chosen to plant, overturning the soil, breaking the hard ground that has been sitting dormant over the winter. This procedure is much like our life when God begins to move us in different directions.

When comparing this metaphor to my life I think it's safe to say this might be my least favorite time of the cycle. Not many people like to be pulled, pushed or coaxed out of their comfort zone. What I didn't realize was those were the times of my greatest growth as a woman. Now, when my life takes a sharp turn, I just buckle my seat belt and get ready for the ride!

I grew up in Iowa, living in the same house most of my life. I never thought of moving away as I had so many friends I had grown up with and extended family that were a big part of my life. As I was going into High School and was elected cheerleader for my freshman year, I was as content as a gopher in soft dirt.

My dad, who was given to restlessness and had been a truck driver for years, traveled to Nevada and found a little town that was for sale. He thought this little Oasis would be a great investment.

I honestly don't remember how long he had been gone from home pursuing this venture before my mother decided we'd take a road trip to Nevada to visit him. My mother loaded all five of her children into the car, heading off to places unknown and planning to be gone for just a couple of weeks. We had no idea what to expect since we had never been to Nevada.

What we found was a tiny gas station, a six-unit motel, a small grocery store, a trailer park, and a four-table restaurant with a bar. Current Creek, Nevada, became home for the next year.

My Grandmother, aunts and uncles in Iowa packed our clothing in big boxes and shipped them to us. I couldn't believe my ears when we were told we weren't going home. I was furious. I kept anticipating that any day we would be heading back to "civilization" and to my familiar surroundings.

There were no homes in Current Creek except for a large house that had been moved into the area and was used to rent rooms to government workers who were measuring sonic booms in the desert. Behind the restaurant and bar were three small trailers that had been there for years. The cook, or some of the hired hands working the ranch, would live in these trailers. The larger trailer was where my parents and three brothers lived. It had only one-bedroom so all three brothers slept on a hide-a-bed in the tiny living quarters. My sister, Linda, and I stayed in a smaller trailer that didn't have the luxury of plumbing. We used the restroom located in the restaurant.

My brothers attended a one-room school down the road that went through the eighth grade while Linda and I drove 108 miles round trip into Ely, Nevada each week day to attend High School. We had two mountain passes to cross between Current Creek and Ely. There were times we would drive over the passes before the plows had cleared snow from the winding roads. We went through two cars that year. One was lost to road conditions, the other taking out a parked car in downtown Ely!

This was the first time I can remember having my soil overturned. I was devastated. I didn't want to leave Iowa. I had so many friends there, and besides I wanted to be a high school cheerleader! I couldn't imagine why my mother would choose going to Nevada to be with my dad over my being a cheerleader! (To say we're self-focused when we're young is an understatement!)

After a year of the "Nevada gamble" we moved to Montana. We stored what few personal belongings we had accumulated over the year into a small camp trailer while we traveled to Iowa to gather a few of our household items we had left behind. We learned that the camp trailer had been vandalized and everything we had stored temporarily had been stolen. I believe it was at this time that I stopped placing value on possessions. We never had many material possessions to begin with, but in less than two years, what we did have was gone, never to be seen again.

I didn't see my friends I had grown up with until I went back for my 10-year class reunion. You can't believe how many former classmates greeted me with, "Where did you go? One day you just disappeared!"

That was the beginning of many changes in my life. It wasn't easy to go through but necessary for me to be where I am today. Looking back, I am thankful for each of those experiences. Every time my soil was overturned, I learned more about life and actually grew stronger in the process.

Would I put my children through the same things? Not if I could help it. It was traumatic to be jerked out of my "soil" like that. Would I have done what my mom did and move my five children to be with their father? I think I would have. I have learned that we can't second-guess what we would have done in situations our parents were in at the time. We're just responsible for our lives today and we are not to judge what others have done in difficult situations.

I still don't like digging up every spring, but in James 1:1-12, I have found comfort on more than one occasion in learning that *through trials comes our greatest opportunity for growth.*

Fast forwarding to a more recent time when my soil was overturned was in 1989. Doug had been employed with a department store for nearly 15 years. It had recently been sold to a large financial institution. Through this transition, several changes were made that were extremely frustrating to all the employees, and several managers quit after years of employment. Doug had planned to retire with this company, feeling secure with our future, which included good benefits and financial incentive.

Two years after the buy-out, Doug couldn't continue to operate with the heavy demands and stress under the new management. After much thought and prayer, we decided to start our own business. This was not an easy decision as Doug is not a risk-taker.

There were so many things to consider. Our daughter, Christina, was graduating from high school at the time, followed by our son Chad a year later. Our financial security would be completely gone as we would be starting a business that was an entirely new concept to Boise. We felt we had explored the opportunities available, deciding this would be the best option for our family.

Doug and I knew we would not have the finances or time to take another vacation with our children once we started our own business. So before he turned in his resignation we planned one last family fling. Christina, Chad and I stopped by the travel bureau and picked up brochures on a Disney Cruise package. When Doug came home from work, we laid out the beautiful brochures and our family began exploring the best way to make this dream vacation a reality.

We knew that financially we couldn't afford this vacation because of the decision to start our own business. So we began figuring the least expensive time we could travel, which was in August, hurricane season! After whittling down unnecessary expenditures and adding all the fixed expenses, we figured the trip would cost $3,300.

We had thirty-three weeks to prepare and save for this trip. I asked everyone to decide how much he or she could contribute to our "vacation fund." With everyone's contributions, we deposited $100 into our vacation account at the bank every week. This agreement was with the understanding that if anyone was unable to fulfill their weekly commitment, a withdrawal would be made from their savings account. This was agreed upon by everyone. Our plan was officially in effect and became a family contract.

At the end of thirty-three weeks we had successfully deposited the entire amount we needed to achieve the goal for our vacation. It was a wonderful experience to work together as a family, planning this once in a lifetime experience. We also planned to drive to North Carolina from Florida to visit my youngest brother, Dennis and his wife Nancy. From there, we would travel to Washington, D.C.

At the time we put the vacation plan into effect, we hadn't made definite decisions on what type of business we would start. We were in the process of investigating several possibilities. We would spend hours in the bookstores, researching Business Magazines and Entrepreneurial publications. Once we made a decision on what kind of business we would start, it was time to take the big step. The time had come to make the big move and go to the bank to secure financing. We were ready to start Automated Blind Cleaning and would be the first ultrasonic blind cleaning service in Boise, Idaho.

I felt like all the tillers were loose on our fields, over-turning everything in sight. There was excitement and anticipation of new beginnings, as well as stark terror! Doug and I would hold our "board meetings" while we were walking our Rottweiler, Cami. We would talk and plan for hours, seeking God's direction in this big decision.

Doug had prepared his letter of resignation, plan-ning to submit it to the company he was working for when we returned from our vacation. All the pieces were beginning to move now, and it was full steam ahead. We designed a logo to be applied to a new company van, and our equipment was en route from the East Coast and would be waiting for us upon our return.

No regrets. Nervous? Oh yes! We were anxious, but it was time for a change. I remember telling Doug how I wished God would send us a telegram letting us know we had made the right decision. We decided to enjoy our dream vacation and deal with everything else when we returned.

We had a wonderful time spending a week at Disney World, Epcot, Disney-MGM Studios, and Kennedy Space Center. We swam at Cocoa Beach, and took a cruise to the Bahamas. It was everything we had imagined and more. Priceless memories we will cherish as a family forever and still recall to this day.

While we were in Washington, D.C., Doug became very ill. We thought it was something he had eaten while on the cruise, or maybe a combination of different foods, humidity and stress of starting a new business. He grew weaker as he was also losing weight and was eager to return to Idaho as his condition continued to worsen.

While we were waiting for our luggage at the Boise airport, our friends who were picking us up told us the company Doug was employed with was closing all four stores in Boise. Doug and I looked at each other and I said, "Well, that is our telegram." We had made the right decision.

Automated Blind Cleaning came into existence on September 1, 1989. There were so many decisions to make. We were not only starting a new business but introducing a new method for cleaning mini blinds that was new to the Boise market. We knew we had to educate the public to the concept of ultrasonic blind cleaning. The stress was constant as we set up our store front and booked trade shows to demonstrate our equipment and method of cleaning blinds.

Doug had not regained his health from our vacation, losing thirty pounds in two and a half months. He assured me it was stress, and that he would be fine. I insisted he see a doctor we have known for years, who practiced preventive medicine.

On November 20, two days after Doug's fortieth birthday, he was diagnosed as having cancer of the pancreas and the prostate. Hearing this diagnosis was a devastating blow. This explained the weight loss, low grade fever, and lack of energy.

I refused to believe we were down for the count. I knew God was in charge of our lives, and that He hadn't brought us through everything we had experienced to have it end like this. Doug was weak physically and emotionally, but he continued to move forward. Our faith grew deeper as we learned more fully not to lean on our own understanding. Proverbs 3:5-6 tells us to *"Trust in the Lord with all your heart and lean not on your own understanding; in all your ways acknowledge Him and He shall direct your paths."*

Doug began unconventional treatment immediately as we assembled prayer support. Our family and friends were not comfortable with the method Doug had chosen. He also sought a conventional evaluation. I won't go into details, but I will say that we were quickly convinced we had made the right choice. Doug responded immediately to the treatment, and within a short period of time was feeling much stronger and was steadily gaining weight.

Doug has had several checkups since and I am pleased to say he remains healthy to this day and cancer free. We are extremely grateful for answered prayer for his healing as well as the timely treatment he received.

I have become stronger each time my soil has been turned. I don't believe God allows uncomfortable situations in our life to punish us, or to watch us squirm. It is called "life" and these circumstances give us opportunity to trust in God and His Word. I have grown stronger as a result of going through, rather than around, our trials.

When there appears to be a storm on the horizon, we have a choice to either lean into the wind or be blown away by it. Remember, a kite rises against the wind, not with it.

If the Lord has begun to move dirt around in your life, go ahead and give Him the entire field. It's really His anyway. He knows the hearts that have been hardened over the years, and is ready to plant a new crop that will produce a harvest you never dreamed possible in your life. Remember, He is a gentleman, and will not trespass. He waits for permission to dig in your dirt as He softens your ground, preparing it for a bountiful harvest.

Always remember how much God loves you and intends to use each situation to prepare you for the plans He has for your life. We want comfort and convenience. He wants our growth for His glory.

Points to Ponder...

Can you recall a time when the soil has been moved around in your life?

How did you respond to the situation?

How did God use the experience?

Chapter 3

Ready to Plant

*A foundation, or root system, is critical to a
healthy plant and to a child.*

We tend to think only children and teenagers go
through "stages." Our entire life consists of
changes, like the seasons. A time for planting, a time for
growing, a time for harvest, and a time for rest. Each
stage is important, lending to the effectiveness of the
following season...each cycle in a sequence to produce
the anticipated harvest.

If we never plant our seeds, we will not reap a harvest. Galatians 6:7 tells us, "Whatever a man sows, this
he will also reap." We are also told in 2 Corinthians 9:6
that "he who sows sparingly shall also reap sparingly;

and he who sows bountifully shall also reap bountifully." According to God's word, the harvest we anticipate is a direct byproduct of the seeds we sow.

Preparing the soil readies the environment that the seed will occupy. This process allows the seed every advantage to be a healthy plant, beginning with a healthy root system, which is essential. Removing any one of the cycles, or seasons, would remove the balance that God intended.

I have a crystal plaque that reads, *"All the flowers of tomorrow are in the seeds of today."* What was planted in our lives as children, is manifested in our lives today.

Our parents did not have the resources that we now have available. I can remember hearing, "Children are to be seen and not heard." This may sound like a harmless phrase, but the seeds that are planted in a young mind will one day bear fruit.

Building a child's value and self-confidence is crucial during the first three to four years of life. Without loving, nurturing interaction with family and friends, the child will grow physically, but will be emotionally unsure of himself, not having the tools to achieve the potential that God has placed within him. The emotional well being of a child was not as much a consideration when I was growing up as it is today.

Would it be fair to criticize the maker of the first electric typewriter for not including a printer? Not at all. The technology was not available to manufacture a printer. I learned to type with a non-electric typewriter, using correction tape and carbon paper when I needed more than one copy. When I was in High School, the manual typewriter evolved to an electric model that had a correction key. Amazing at the time. When I originally came to McCall to begin work on this book, my husband bought me a state of the art Word Processor. At the time of this writing, May 20, 2011, I am back in McCall, in the same condo where I began this book, sitting at the same table, using an Apple laptop, nineteen years later.

Parenting techniques have evolved over the years as well. I believe there is an awareness we have learned in building emotional stability. I don't think it would be wise to use all the same tools our parents used, especially if we are limping through life as a result of techniques used in our childhood. It is important to implement the disciplines that encouraged strong character and good work ethic that perhaps our parents instilled in us. The key is not to overlook the opportunities to encourage good behavior as the child maneuvers the obstacles that are inevitable in their formative years.

Farmers today plant the same seed that has been used for generations. However you don't see many farmers in the fields with horse drawn plows. The same is true with children. Babies have not changed. God hasn't added new parts, but the way in which we raise and nurture children has changed as we draw from our experiences and those of others. It is recognizing that relationships, like our technology, have evolved.

Root systems are crucial in producing strong, healthy plants capable of weathering the elements and enabling the production of prolific fruit. The roots need oxygen and proper nutrition, which includes water. This is a delicate balance, which is often difficult when growing a garden, much less raising children.

As an adult I can look back upon my life and see situations and circumstances where I was confused and even angry. I didn't like the fact that my father was gone most of the time. I didn't understand why he would leave every time we would move to a different state to be with him. I didn't know why he would abandon my mother to raise five children by herself. I didn't like the idea that maybe we weren't worth his time or attention. As a child, I didn't have choices about my life. However, I can remember thinking at a young age that one day I would have 'choices'.

"Choose for you and your household whom you will serve" (Joshua 24:15), is engraved on a wall plaque that has hung in our home for years. It is a reminder of the most important choice I have made personally and one that would affect all my choices in the future.

Adults who have suffered physical or sexual abuse, no longer have to live with the guilt or shame that has become their identity. We can grow bitter or we can grow better. We can crawl under our experiences and let them rob us of our future, or we can climb on top of them, giving us a better vantage point, growing in spite of them. It becomes our choice to turn those bad experiences into mulch and use it for fertilizer for next year's crop!

Isaiah 43:18...*"Do not call to mind the former things, or ponder things of the past. Behold, I will do something new. Now it will spring forth; will you not be aware of it? I will even make a roadway in the wilderness, rivers in the desert."*

There is one thing certain that we all have in common, not one of us can relive our past. If we spend our time looking at yesterday's pain and failures, or basking in yesterday's accomplishments and achievements, we will miss tomorrow's opportunities that are opening up for us today. We will not recognize the *"roadway in the wilderness or river in the desert"* that the Lord has prepared for us.

I believe the best thing you can do for your children is to forgive their grandparents and those who may have abused or disappointed you. The choice not to forgive keeps us in bondage and contaminates other relationships in our lives. The relationship we have with our parents is a primary relationship. It is how we learn to relate to others outside our family. Apart from our relationship with God, our relationship with our parents begins to establish a mindset which influences the person we are today.

Does this mean I am suggesting I have to like everything about my childhood and approve of parenting techniques that were used? That is not what I'm implying. What I am saying is that the roots we have will determine the fruit we will produce. What do you want your harvest to be like? We can become an assembly line of repeating weaknesses, passing them on from generation to generation. The chain can be broken, and your entire family will benefit.

If there was alcohol abuse, physical abuse, verbal abuse, sexual abuse, emotional abuse, or drug abuse in your home as a child, are you overlooking it in your home today? Denial is not just a river in Egypt! Perhaps denial has been the only means you can handle difficult situations. It will appear in other behaviors until you reprocess it properly as an adult. Until that time, it will cast a shadow on your family today. Don't rob them of a healthy future by not establishing a good environment for them to grow.

When I pick up our mail each day it is usually dominated by "junk mail." I normally automatically just toss it in the garbage. If I were to ask one of my grandchildren to get the mail, they wouldn't recognize the "junk mail" from the bills or important correspondence. It is the same idea when it comes to sorting through the "junk mail" from our childhood. What we have set aside and held on to all these years needs to be tossed. At the time it was huge and even appeared to be something we needed to keep. Even to the point of rehearsing it and retelling it to others so we would never forget. Been there, done that. Looking back as an adult, it is time to toss it. We get good at what we rehearse. We can memorize our misery or rehearse our righteousness that we have in Christ.

I taught a Jr. and Sr. High Sunday school class at our church. I had been doing a lesson on forgiveness as we were discussing relationships with our parents. My objective was to help the class be more understanding and forgiving of their parents.

One Sunday as the youth came into class, I handed them each a piece of paper, asking them to write items they would like to have. After much thought and more than a few comments, they turned in the papers, listing their heart's desires.

I told them to take their lists home and to bring the things they had written in class with them the following Sunday. I told them they would be able to use the back parking lot if they needed room to park the sports cars, trucks, boats, etc. They expressed obvious disbelief at my request, as some of the class said they couldn't get the things they had listed. I told them it would be fine with me if they borrowed them from their parents, or they could even have an extra week to accumulate the objects.

"I don't have any way of getting these things, my parents can't get them either," replied one of the boys. "There's no way my parents could ever come up with anything on my list, they've never even owned a new car," replied another.

Once the conversation quieted, I explained to them that the emotional support the young people wanted or needed was perhaps something their parents did not possess as well. Possibly their parents had never been given approval as a child, never having felt loved or appreciated themselves.

By making an effort to understand circumstances and to forgive the "shade" that has blocked our growth as children, we can then make the choice to move on with our lives.

The young people in our class became very quiet as they began to see their parents in a different light. God tells us to honor our parents. This doesn't mean we always respect them. They are human, and there are times when we don't respect what they do or say. However, forgiveness is a gift you give yourself, and it is certainly a gift that goes on giving to the next generation. Forgiveness is a choice that only we can make and the decision to forgive always gives way to freedom.

Jesus extended forgiveness to us as He died on the cross to pay for our sins. When we choose not to forgive others, we withhold the forgiveness that God offers us.

Jesus tells us in Matthew 6:14-15, *"For if you forgive men for their transgressions, your heavenly Father will also forgive you. But if you do not forgive men, then your Father will not forgive your transgressions."*

A difficult truth to embrace, but only through forgiving others can we walk in the freedom God intended for our lives.

Fathers who leave a void in a child's life will unknowingly cause the child to seek fulfillment elsewhere. Unfortunately, there are many young men that step up to the altar on their wedding day to say, "I do," and later realize, "they can't."

The beautiful bride that is all aglow will eventually try to stuff her husband into the void left in her heart by her father's absence. She will expect her husband to make up for all the years of rejection she has accumulated and hold him responsible for the emptiness she continues to feel.

If it sounds like I am speaking from experience, I am. A few years into my marriage to Doug I began to realize I was doing this to my husband. I had unknowingly placed emotional expectations on Doug that were unfair. That is when I knew I needed a relationship with my dad. There had to be a separate identity for these two men in my life.

As I mentioned earlier, when I was a child my father was busy chasing dreams. He had a very creative mind, which opened the door to him becoming an inventor. He was also a mechanic, a truck driver as well as a stock car driver.

Over the years dad modified several stock cars that he would drive Friday, Saturday and Sunday nights throughout the summer. He traveled to Minnesota, South Dakota as well as our home state of Iowa. Although my mother was not necessarily fond of dad's racing, she would pack all five of us children into the station wagon, along with a supply of bologna sandwiches and potato chips, following our dad as he pursued his dream.

Unrelated to racing, we later followed our dad to Nevada and eventually to Montana. It was during this time that my dad was developing a prototype of a carburetor which was fuel-efficient and emissions friendly. While we were enrolled in school in Montana, dad had migrated to California. His newest venture was testing the carburetor he was developing on several makes of automobiles.

My mother, who was always trying to keep the family together, loaded us all up once again and headed to San Bernardino for the summer. My dad was renting a house so the family was temporarily together again.

My brother, Duane, worked with dad in the research lab, installing the carburetors into a variety of different makes of cars. These test cars would be monitored, determining their fuel efficiency as well as the level of fuel emissions.

My sister, Linda, and I were on the team of drivers who were responsible for putting over 100,000 miles on the cars, driving twelve hour shifts. The car was to run 24-7 to gather the data necessary for recording the success of the carburetor. When our shift was over, the other person scheduled would get behind the wheel and drive for the next 12 hours.

I was fifteen at the time and did not have a driver's license. This didn't keep me from driving to Las Vegas, Nevada from San Bernardino, California by myself or to navigate the freeways in Southern California. I was asked several times to pick up men flying into the L.A.

airportthat were interested in the research that was taking place.

When two of the cars needed more miles for final testing, my dad decided a quick run to Montana and back would do the trick. A big request and huge responsibility for me and my sister. Especially considering we were to drive the 1,125 miles to Hamilton, Montana, which took 16 hours, without stopping for sleep!

Looking back, recalling this time in my life and the responsibility my dad gave me at such a young age, staggers my mind. I chose to forgive my dad years ago for the times he had disappointed me, as I continued to pursue a relationship with him. I knew it would not be an ideal relationship, which is subjective, but would be a relationship based on my being willing to accept whatever he had to offer.

Helping our children to develop strong, healthy roots enables them to reach unlimited growth above the ground. To encourage the growth, we must give them value as a person, not just on performances. Their value has to come from an unconditional love based upon who they are, not on what they can do. If our children only see our approval after the completion of a chore, or at the end of a performance, they will not develop the roots of self-value.

God's love for us is not based on *performance* and our salvation is not based on *works*. When the only approval children see is related to performance or works, they will not be able to rest in knowing that God loves them unconditionally. There is nothing we can do to add to or take away from the value that God places on us. Why would we offer our children anything less?

My father was a very creative man. He was intelligent and constantly thinking of how he could make something better. His approval was hard to acquire. Because he was not free with his compliments, I didn't feel as if I could ever please him. He would speak of my accomplishments to others, but would not express his approval to me.

I felt my father's approval was based on performance, and I was never sure of the score. Can you imagine going through school, studying, getting your homework assignments in on time, and participating in class, yet never knowing what grade you had earned?

That is how I felt with my father. I never knew what my grade was with him.

My mother was very supportive of me, giving me responsibilities that would indicate that she had confidence in my abilities to do whatever she would ask. She took her role as a mother very seriously and always wanted us to be together as a family. I watched my mom go through difficult situations as she worked very hard providing for her five children.

My father and I had a different relationship before he died May 3, 2009. It was very open, and we would talk on the phone quite often. Our conversations were centered on relationships and not accomplishments. I still don't know what my grade was with my dad, but it didn't matter to me anymore. I knew he loved me.

Improving and renewing relationships has been on my heart for years. Just because a plant is old doesn't mean you can't give the root system a little oxygen, breathing new life into the plant. You can take a plant that appears near death and unproductive, completely out of its old used-up soil. After rinsing the roots in tepid water you can then transplant the bedraggled plant into a larger pot with new soil.

This is what happens when we allow Jesus to be our gardener. It feels good to be in a new pot with fresh soil, and to be watered with "living water." The fruit that is produced in lives we live and people we touch, will be a harvest that will benefit others for generations.

I heard a story on the radio one morning that I would like to share... There was once a man who had a beautiful apple orchard. People would travel for miles to buy the huge, juicy, red apples that his orchard produced. One day a regular customer noticed the man planting trees across the highway from his existing orchard. The customer was curious, asking the man why he was planting a new orchard when he had always harvested such beautiful apples.

"I was so caught up in the fruit from the orchard and all the work involved with the fruit stand that I neglected the trees that were producing the fruit. Over years of neglect, the trees in my orchard were dying," replied the man sadly.

Like the man and his orchard, sometimes we only recognize accomplishments and fail to see the person who is crying out for love and appreciation. We need to appreciate the tree from which the fruit is grown, the person or child behind the accomplishments.

The real fruit begins in the roots that we give our children. A solid foundation of confidence is what is essential to let them go. It is like taking the guide wires off a new tree at the proper time. When we have helped them establish a healthy root system, we know the storms will come, but we have taught them to lean into the wind, becoming strong as a result.

When I stopped going to the empty well and realized the source that I had available to me, the Living Water that the Bible speaks of, I was able to forgive my father for the times in my life that he had been absent. It was then that I could release him from my expectations. I have discovered over the years that disappointment is often a by-product of unrealistic expectation.

When we give our children roots, I don't believe this means a house with a wrap-around porch and a garden out back. If this is part of your life story, that's a bonus.

The roots I'm talking about are who they are as people, experiencing the unconditional love that you have for them. I believe this is accomplished by your investment of time more than anything else.

They need to know that you enjoy spending time with them. They need to have you listen with your eyes as well as your ears. They need to know you are genuinely interested in the challenges that they are facing, regardless how trivial it may seem at the time. They need to know that even if they fail miserably on a test, on the playing field, or in the band that you are still proud of them for the effort they invested. Each time you have the opportunity to extend your arms when they feel undeserving, you will be offering them the biggest shot of "Miracle Grow" that will strengthen their root system like nothing else.

We were not able to give our children the security of a childhood home that would have a growth chart on a threshold, carefully recorded from the time they could stand on their own. By the time we had been married nine years, we had moved fourteen times! I began to develop a rash around cardboard boxes!

One Christmas I considered making wall samplers for our siblings of homes that they had raised their children in. I thought I would make our family a sampler of a U-Haul truck since our address was constantly changing.

If roots were a house where you grew up, knowing several generations of family and neighbors up and down the block, then our children wouldn't have a root system to hold them in place.

Doug spent two years in the US Army, and was stationed in Ft. Hood, Texas. I was able to go with him for the entire two years. Our children were both born during his time in Texas. The total hospital bill for Christina's delivery was $7.00. Our bill for Chad sixteen months later was $25.00. We bought our first dog, Arnie, out of a trunk of a car in a parking lot for $35.00. What a deal. A family, complete with a pet, for $67.00!

Doug and I would talk for hours about how we were going to raise these precious children. All our time and attention was focused on Christina and Chad. I believe with all my heart that this is where the root system is crucial. We delighted in every new development they experienced. The trip to a nearby park was a regular routine, as well as rides in the car with picnics, and playing "hide and go seek".

Doug is an awesome father and was very involved with our children as babies. He was not above any of the daily routine that comes with the territory, including several pretty nasty clean up details. We were total rookies as parents and had a lot to learn. We maintain that our children survived in spite of us, not because of us!

Christina had a problem going to sleep at night. I don't want to use the word spoiled here, but it could apply. We made many mistakes when it came to bedtime routines. We both loved to rock our babies to sleep. This of course created an inability for them to relax on their own and fall to sleep naturally. There were times when Christina would wake up at three or four in the morning. She would cry so hard that she would vomit. Doug and I would flip a coin. One would clean the bedding, the other would tend to Christina. Eventually Doug would take his pillow, lie down in the middle of her room and let her crawl and play until she would finally lie down next to her daddy and fall asleep.

I would like to say that we recognized our error and corrected it with Chad. However, his sleeping schedule was even worse. I don't think he slept through the night until he was three. Our children always knew they were welcome on our laps, riding daddy's leg like a horse, and going for piggyback rides. As they grew, we logged many hours with all the pillows in the house piled in the middle of the floor giggling, watching movies and playing board games. We have always enjoyed their company, and to this day, I would have a difficult time choosing a favorite age as they were growing up.

When Doug got out of the service we headed for Montana, enjoying the opportunity to live closer to our families. Shortly after we thought we were settled for a time, Doug was transferred to Boise, Idaho with C.R. Anthony's Department store.

We had never been to Boise but were up for the adventure of yet another town to call home. We enjoyed Boise immediately, making close friends as our children were now entering school. I finished Cosmetology

School and was in the process of testing for my license. I was taking a practice board exam when I was told I had a phone call.

"I have been offered the store in Glendive, Montana and have accepted the offer," Doug said nervously.

"When do they need you to be there?" I asked.

"As soon as I hang up the phone, I'm going to get the U-Haul," was his hurried reply.

We were on the road the next morning at 6:00 a.m. Another quick move, and another new adventure. We had discussed previously that we were open to a transfer if Doug was offered a management position.

The store in Glendive had so many problems that were a tremendous challenge for a new manager. Doug turned it around in just a matter of months. It left us both emotionally and financially drained. Doug was cashing in the savings bonds that his mother bought for him when his father died, to buy groceries. Have you heard the saying, 'We were so broke we couldn't afford to pay attention?' That pretty much described our financial situation.

We lived in a motel for sixteen days with a U-Haul loaded with all our earthly possessions. Glendive had become a boom town with all the oil drilling leaving no housing available. We finally located a mobile home that had been stored in a farm field. It was not only filthy, but everything that could leak, did leak. Dead mice lay everywhere. The home we had been renting in Boise was a two bedroom with a basement. Moving into this mobile home was like putting ten pounds of flour into a five-pound bag!

Doug and I had a good marriage, two beautiful children, health, and a good job. However, I began to sense something missing. I realized I had a piece missing in my life puzzle. Have you ever completed a jigsaw puzzle only to discover there is a piece missing? You can make out the content but it is just not completed.

Doug and I had both gone to church when we were young but I had not attended church since I left Iowa. When Christina and Chad were six and five, I thought we needed to take them to Sunday School so they could learn the songs I sang as a child. What I didn't realize was how much I needed this for myself. The Lord draws the children to Himself, and I'm sure it is His plan that the adults will follow. The seeds our parents had planted by sending us to Sunday School had taken hold and were beginning to sprout.

All the moves were starting to affect me. I became depressed and didn't leave the mobile home for days at a time. The winter in Glendive was brutal with temperatures dipping to thirty-four below zero. The engine heater on our car caught fire which left us without a vehicle in the dead of winter.

It was during this time that I was flipping through the television channels and ran across the PTL program. At first I flipped past it, but had to go back and take another look at the woman that was crying, who happened to be Tammy Faye Baker. I had no idea who she was but I kept looking at her wondering if she was for real. (Just being honest.)

I began listening to what Tammy Faye was saying with my ears instead of judging her with my eyes. My heart was so ready to receive what my ears were hearing. She spoke of the love of Jesus who would never leave us or forsake us. I felt as though I was dying of thirst and she was offering me a drink of "Living Water." I began to cry as the truth of her words went deep into the empty place in my heart that only Jesus could fill.

I went to the phone, dialing the number on the bottom of the screen and accepted Jesus into my life as my Savior as a prayer counselor led me in prayer. I can remember a sense of peace as the words I had spoken were filling my heart and my mind. I continued to listen to the show and savored every word I was hearing.

When Doug came home from work, I wasn't sure how to tell him what I had done. I didn't want anything to take away the peace that I had experienced.

That evening I was giving him a haircut and just "happened" to turn the television to the PTL program. He wasn't sure what he was watching and when he saw Tammy Faye he began to make a comment. I encouraged him to listen to what she was saying and turned his chair away from the television as I continued cutting his hair.

After that day, church had a different affect on my life. I couldn't get enough of the teachings. Our pastor and his wife agreed to do a Bible Study with Doug and me and Doug's bookkeeper and her husband every week. We went through the book of John slowly and will always be grateful for the time our Pastor and his wife took to get us started on this life long journey.

Doug was transferred back to Boise exactly one year from the time we had arrived in Glendive. We immediately began looking for a church. A client told me about a church he had been attending and really enjoyed. We visited Trinity Fellowship and immediately knew this was a church we wanted to attend on a regular basis. We attended every Sunday and began to grow in understanding God's Word. We eventually hosted a Bible Study in our home with Pastor Hank teaching and our good friend Mike leading our group in worship. Our children were exposed to this time of study and worship and would often join us, especially when we would break out the refreshments.

One Sunday as our family was getting ready for church, Chad announced that he didn't feel like going. I believe he was eleven. I knew this day would come, so I said, "Okay, maybe Christina would like to skip church today as well." She jumped at the option to stay home, so Doug and I went to church by ourselves for the first time. After the service we went out for breakfast and took a ride. The kids felt as if they had missed out and were a bit bored just sitting at home.

A few weeks later Chad made the same announcement, that he didn't want to go to church. When I asked him why he didn't want to go, he replied, "I heard you tell someone that when your kids got old enough to decide for themselves, that you wouldn't make them go to church anymore."

"Chad, are you old enough to drive?" I asked.

"No, of course I'm not old enough to drive," he replied.

I then asked curiously, "Are you old enough to vote, Chad?" Again his answer was no. Finally I asked, "Chad, can you decide for yourself if you want to attend school?"

He never said a word. Three strikes and he was out! I suggested that he shower. I explained to him the vows we had made the day he was baptized at the age of five. I told Chad that I wasn't going to stand before God one day and have Him ask me why I let my eleven year old son talk me out of a covenant I had made with Him.

Every time Chad or Christina witnesses a baby dedication, they hear again the commitment the parents are making, to raise their child in an understanding and knowledge of the Lord.

Of all the roots we have given our children, I feel the most significant ones have been the ones in the Lord. They both asked Jesus into their hearts at a Billy Graham Crusade in Boise. Doug and I were counselors for the crusade, so our children attended each night as well. We couldn't sit with them since we were assigned seats with other counselors.

During one of the last evenings we spotted both Christina and Chad with counselors, making a commitment to the Lord. Chad and Christina were each given a little booklet that explained the commitment they had just made to Jesus in words they could understand. I'm not going to tell you they are perfect, but I can tell you they are saved. Both of them know where they will spend eternity. John 3:16 tells us that *"God so loved the world that He gave his only Son so that whoever believes in Him should not perish but will have eternal life."*

What is your root system like? I encourage you not to feel despair if you were planted in poor soil and have cutworms eating away at your fragile roots. As long as you realize you don't have to stay in that worn out soil. You are the one who can pick up roots and move to higher ground and better soil. Remember that you have to make the first move. God is a gentleman. He will not push Himself on you, but waits patiently.

I can remember lying in my Grandmother Clifford's bed when I was a child. I would look at the picture of Jesus knocking on a heavy wooden door. I loved that picture and didn't realize until I was an adult that there was no handle on the outside of the door. The only way Jesus could enter was if the door was opened from the inside. That door represents our heart. He wants to come live in our hearts no matter what the condition.

Revelation 3:20 had new meaning as Jesus says, *"Behold! I stand at the door and knock; if anyone hears my voice and opens the door, I will come in to him..."*

He wants us to experience His Presence in our lives, enabling us to live lives that we could never imagine. It's your life, and your choice.

Points to ponder...

Is there a person in your life that you have refused to forgive?

How has your decision not to forgive affected your life?

Are there people in your life that you have disappointed or hurt?

When we receive forgiveness from God, we were told to offer it to others.

(Matthew 6:15, Luke 6:37)

Forgiveness is not a suggestion, it is the foundation for living a life pleasing to God.

Chapter 4

Realizing the Light

I began to believe with my heart instead of my head who Jesus was in my life.

Have you ever had a house or patio plant that looked great in the nursery or flower shop, but when it took up residence in your home, it was a sure death sentence? Perhaps one that turned into a 'silk plant wanna-be,' never producing a new leaf or blossom? I've had a few of these experiences, especially with outdoor plants.

Plants require soil for support, water, light, oxygen and nutrition. In our quest for beautiful plants we often over-water, causing its poor roots to rot as they are drowned by not having enough oxygen.

We believe that our plants will receive all the nutrition they need from the dirt we've placed them in. The primary purpose of the dirt is to support the plant. Nutrients need to be added gradually over the life of the plant.

We often place our new plant in full sun or full shade and expect them to do as well as in the ideal greenhouse environment we originally bought them from. Those plants had originally been pampered, pruned and pesticide protected. They had also been given the proper humidity, enabling the plants to thrive while producing gorgeous blooms.

On more than one occasion, I have brought home beautiful plants I just described, jerked out last year's failures from the planters, and arranged this year's hopefuls in the same exhausted dirt and insect infested potting soil. Does anyone else practice this ritual?

The most consistent part of this routine is when I hold my husband responsible for my plants not blooming! Now I'm not proud to reveal this to you, but whether spoken or unspoken, I have held him responsible! In my mind, I have assigned him the position of "plant guard." I have found this works well for me, because I no longer have to feel responsible for not preparing a proper environment for the plants. I have at times even blamed our dogs for my not having beautiful plants in the back yard. However, except for the year that Cami was a puppy, and would pick a bouquet of petunias for me nearly every day, she has never bothered my plants.

Doug has christened me the "queen of excuses," and rightfully so. I can usually give you an excuse for why I do something before you will have the question out of your mouth. Justifying my actions had always been the way I operated.

Much like the plants we bring home from the garden shop are the expectations for our children when we bring them home from the hospital. We envision our plants as the mature, beautiful specimens we have seen in gardening magazines, reproducing beautiful blossoms from year to year.

However, just as the plants are no longer in the ideal environment, protected from every outside insect invasion or unintended lack of watering, children sometimes meet the same demise. No matter how well intended we are as parents, a predator can still find its way to our children.

I have been so frustrated with the bud worms that show up every year and pilfer my outdoor potted plants. I don't know why they favor my plants, sucking the life out of the tiny buds that are just beginning to open.

I finally found a bud worm in the act of munching on a newly formed petunia bud. I couldn't believe how camouflaged they are, blending in so perfectly, looking just like the stems of the flowers they are destroying.

I even said out loud when I spotted the persistent pest, "God, whose side are you on here? Bright orange would have been a good choice of colors for these nasty predators. At least I could identify the bud worms, protecting these tender plants from their ravaging affect on my beautiful plants!"

It occurred to me that these worms are much like the predators that prey upon our children. We don't always recognize them or even have reason to be suspicious in most cases. They are much like the bud worm that blends into the environment, not drawing any attention to itself. Quietly sucking the life out of the flower buds, not allowing them to develop into the blooms that were anticipated.

I was a very young girl when a neighbor boy began spending far too much time with children much younger than himself. We had a playhouse in our yard where we would spend hours playing with our siblings and neighborhood children. This playhouse also provided an opportunity for our neighbor's son to be inappropriate as he began to find more occasions to separate me away from the safety and watchful eye of my family.

A ride with him on his bike around the block would end up in a cluster of lilac bushes. The bushes created a camouflage for the molestation that took place. His request filled me with curiosity, confusion and shame. I don't recall what was said exactly, but I do know it was not something I could tell my mother.

One afternoon his mother came looking for him and found him in our playhouse. There were words that revealed she had caught him in the act. I don't believe I ever saw him again.

For years I put the memory of playhouses, bike rides with lilac bushes and corners in garages out of my mind.

Looking back, I believe the Lord protected me from further violation by prompting his mother to investigate at the appropriate time.

Just like the bud worm I mentioned earlier, the predator that was a neighbor boy, was not 'out of place,' but was most certainly 'out of line.' It was a person that was trusted and was part of the environment of the neighborhood, not a stranger lurking in the bushes.

Children who are just learning about life can become bewildered by such encounters that often go on for years in their lives. It becomes a dark place of shame and guilt that often expresses itself in a variety of behaviors and mind sets.

When I realized my backside was shaded, you can't imagine how many people or situations I held responsible. I was quite comfortable where I stood. I just wanted Doug to hold a grow light on me so I could have the best of both worlds. I wanted the security of standing close to Doug without the risk of failure should I try something new. Real growth needs real light.

The impact of that phone call to PTL years ago still resonates in my life today. The "Light" that I accepted into my heart that day, forever changed my life. I heard, for the first time with my heart instead of my ears, that Jesus was the Light of the world. I learned that He was the Son of God, and that He had died on the cross for me and for all my sins... past, present and future. Jesus was buried, and three days later He arose from the dead, defeating Satan and the power he had against me. Jesus ascended to heaven to prepare a place for me to live with Him for all eternity.

Jesus left me the Holy Spirit, who is my constant source of comfort and guidance, so I would never be alone. I also learned that salvation is a gift that can't be earned, and isn't deserved by anyone.

Paul speaks of this amazing grace that was offered in Ephesians 2:8-9 when he says, *"For by grace you have been saved through faith; and that was not of yourselves but a gift from God; not as a result of works so that no one could boast."* This gift of grace, undeserved favor, was offered to me if I chose to accept Jesus as my Lord and Savior. He picked up all the blame, all the excuses, all my anger, all my disappointments, all the guilt, all my weaknesses, and carried them to the cross with Him.

He knew me from the moment that I was conceived (Psalm 139:13-18). He loves me and constantly thinks about me. He was willing to give everything for me, even to die on a cross for me. He knew that I could never enter Heaven without Him. In John 14:6 Jesus says, *"I am the way, the truth, and the life. No one can come to the Father except through Me."*

The light I had in my life before I knew Jesus had kept me alive, but I didn't grow. My roots were shallow, my strength was my own, and my identity was in my circumstances. Once I received this new "Light," my roots were planted in trust, my strength was that of the Lord and His promises, and my new identity is that I am a child of God. I belong to a royal family. I am a child of the King of Kings!

Does this mean that I can do anything I want and not be held responsible? Not at all. I am responsible to the Lord. I didn't say I was perfect, I said I was forgiven. He knows my heart and my motives. When I make wrong choices, I know I am out of His will. It's not a good feeling, knowing you are being disobedient. I feel uneasiness and disharmony inside me when I am out of His will. I have an uneasiness inside me when I say things I shouldn't say or compromise my position, not wanting to create controversy.

The sun, which plants so desperately need, is such a welcome guest in our home. My spirits are lifted each morning as I open the blinds to allow the light to flood into the room.

Have you ever noticed in the spring, when the sun shines so brightly, how it reveals how dirty your windows and blinds have become over the winter? This is what happened to me when Jesus began to shine His light into my life. Things that didn't seem so bad before began to be distasteful to me. I wasn't comfortable in certain environments, and around off-color conversations that I would have participated in before I became exposed to this new Light. I was uncomfortable with thoughts and feelings that I had always justified before.

Being a Christian doesn't keep me from sinning, it just takes the enjoyment out of it! You can tilt your blinds for a while, and try to filter the light so that things won't look so bad. Eventually, you realize it is your choice and yours alone. You can open your blinds or keep them closed. When I asked Jesus into my life, I would have been disappointed with anything less than exposure of my "dust bunnies."

In John 8:12, Jesus said, *"I am the light of the world; he who follows Me shall not walk in the darkness, but shall have the light of life."* Light and darkness cannot occupy the same space.

I don't know anyone who would dust their furniture in the dark, or sweep the floor with the lights off. If you hired a cleaning service and they came in and hit a few high spots and left, I'm sure you wouldn't be pleased. Don't expect any less when Jesus takes up residence in your life, rolls up His sleeves, and mucks the place out!

When He begins to clean, He doesn't put up with junk drawers very long. When He first moved in, there was an excitement with this new guest. I showed Him around, but a new guest doesn't usually snoop in your drawers or closets. The difference between Jesus and just another guest is that He doesn't want to just expose these areas as needing attention. He wants to clean them out for you! What a deal!

Several years ago, Doug invited me to go on a business trip to Oklahoma City for C.R. Anthony's annual convention. I was so excited as we made plans to have Doug's mother, Helen, come down from Montana to spend the week with Christina and Chad. Helen likes to clean. She is always wiping something down or polishing the toaster or refrigerator. This used to intimidate me. Because I was insecure at that time in my life, I interpreted her to be insinuating that I was not a good housekeeper. She would even get out Q-tips and clean the little wheel on the can opener!

I would be exhausted when I knew she was coming, because I wanted her to know what a wonderful little homemaker I was. This was my identity, to be a June Cleaver, minus the pumps and pearls! I would even clean the inside of my washing machine and dishwasher when I knew she was coming. Right before she would arrive, I would hurry and check the kid's ears because she had an inexhaustible supply of Q-tips!

You cannot believe the freedom and relief I felt when I realized she wasn't being disapproving of me when she did this polishing and cleaning. She just liked doing it. She didn't mean it as an insult, and would have been disappointed if she didn't have something to ding out during her visits.

When I was stocking the kitchen for the week we were to be gone, I was sure to buy oven cleaner, plenty of ammonia, cleanser, and a new box of Q-tips. I even had a fresh supply of cleaning rags for her arrival. It was great to come home to a squeaky-clean house. In fact, she took apart the exhaust hood over the stove, and cleaned it so well that it did squeak!

She didn't come to pick apart the way I cleaned house, or cared for our children. She came to help. Some mothers-in-laws come with their white gloves to expose your dust and grime. Helen came with her rubber gloves to get into the grimy corners that I don't like to clean because it gave her great satisfaction in doing it.

That's the way Jesus is. He gets into the darkest attics and dampest cellars and cleans them out for us. He dumps the junk mail that has piled up and cleans the grimy areas that are overwhelming for us to tackle. He knows if we could do it ourselves, we would have done so by now.

I have also learned that He knows what we are capable of and will not do anything we are able to do for ourselves. He is not interested in stifling our growth, but strengthening us for His glory.

The secret is that we have to give Him permission to do this spring-cleaning. I allowed Him to wander around for quite some time, assuring Him that I was going to get to certain things that I knew needed attention. He was patient with me to get comfortable with His "cleaning service," allowing me to progress through the process as my trust in Him continued to grow.

If you are wondering if I've cleaned every hall closet, and gone through every junk drawer, I haven't. Even if I had at one time, we all know it is a continual process as long as we live in the house. So as long as we're alive, there will always be upkeep on the place as life has a way of accumulating clutter.

Once I began to breathe cleaner air as a result of blowing a few cobwebs out, I could understand how a plant must feel when we remove the dust from its leaves. I couldn't wait to share this refreshing revelation with my family. I wanted them to experience Jesus in the same way I had come to know Him.

When Christina and Chad were young teenagers we planned a weekend in McCall to enjoy spending time by the fire, playing board games and cross country skiing. I wanted to be prepared so I had all the materials I needed to direct their eyes, mind and heart to the Jesus who had become so important in my life. I'm not sure if bringing workbooks along was such a good idea.

I could tell Doug and the children were being tolerant of me as my plan was beginning to unravel. As badly as I wanted them to thirst for things of God like a deer with a new salt lick, I knew I was losing ground fast. I'm so glad God uses a different approach!

After an aborted attempt to inject Jesus into their every thought, we decided to go cross-country skiing at Ponderosa State Park. We all needed to work off a little frustration and I needed to let go of my unrealistic expectations. Our destination was the highest point in the park. I chose not to take Doug's 'short cut' and ended up on a separate trail by myself.

It had begun to snow gently with huge snowflakes that made the view from every direction look like a Thomas Kinkade Christmas card. Everything was covered with several inches of white fluffy snow that just took my breath away. As I reached the top of the point, looking over the lake into town, I was in awe of the beauty that surrounded me. It was so still I could hear my heart beat, and nothing else. I said out loud, "Oh God, this is so beautiful, it's like there is no one here except You and me."

It was as if I heard God say, "Yes LaDonna, just you and Me. Not you and Doug and Me. Not you, Christina, Chad and Me. Just you and Me. I will take it from here. They will seek to know Me more intimately in their time, not in yours."

As these thoughts were going through my mind I noticed Doug, Christina and Chad were skiing up the road to the point where I was standing. They didn't arrive together. They came one at a time. We all stood and admired the view. We'd taken different trails, but we all ended up at the same location.

When we returned to the condo and were all snuggled down for the evening, I told my family the thoughts I had while standing on that point by myself. I told my children that it was my responsibility to introduce them to Jesus, but their relationship with Him was their responsibility. I don't honestly recall but I think there were a few "high fives" and a round of hot chocolate and a board game with lots of laughter and sighs of relief!

When you flip on the light switch in a dark room, you have unleashed an amazing amount of power from the source of electricity that is directly connected to the switch. You acquire a similar power in your life when you tap into the "Light of Jesus."

You have within you the same power that raised Jesus from the dead, the Holy Spirit. We usually stumble around in the dark, not recognizing we have permission to turn the switch on in our lives that will access an illumination that will truly flood our lives with hope for our future.

Points to Ponder...

Where is your light coming from in your life?

Is it causing you to grow, or is it just keeping you alive?

Chapter 5

Harvest Time

A time of reaping what we have sowed.

Autumn is a beautiful season. The air is crisp in the morning, giving way to the balmy warm afternoons. The incredible colors of nature become remarkably vivid in hues of golds and crimson reds.

The fields and orchards have been harvested as fruit and vegetable stands appear on nearly every corner. It's a time of mixed emotions. Celebration that the crops are mature and healthy, but also knowing there is a time of dormancy that lays ahead.

As parents, Doug and I have experienced a time of harvest in our lives. We invested a tremendous amount of love and time into our two precious children, Christina and Chad. I wouldn't trade the challenges or trials as each situation strengthened us as a family. It was through the challenges that we had the opportunity to parent and to stand beside our children with love and support.

Just as a farmer prepares his field for the crop to be planted, we as parents are responsible to prepare an environment for our children to grow into a love and understanding of who God is.

The book of Hosea speaks of how necessary it is to use the plow to break up the hard ground in chapter 10. *"Plant the good seeds of righteousness, and you will harvest a crop of love. Plow up the hard ground of your hearts for now is the time to seek the Lord that He may come and shower righteousness upon you."*

God also reminds me that we may plant the seeds by sharing the Lord with our children or those around us, but He may use others to water the seeds we planted over the years.

In 1 Corinthians 3:6 we are reminded that *it is God who causes the growth* and that we are *His field.*

As we have watched our children grow through the seasons, they have observed growth in both my husband and myself. When they were teenagers, we told them that we had never been parents of teenagers before, but we had obviously been teenagers. We were all experiencing something new at the same time. We would all navigate through this unfamiliar territory and learn from one another with cooperation and respect.

When our children were going into Jr. High, we were attending a Bible Study. One evening it was decided to spend the entire time praying for one another's prayer needs. When it was my turn, I asked for wisdom for raising our children through the teenage years. God has been so faithful as He has given me insight and discernment for every situation.

It is now June of 2011 and I am back in McCall to put the finishing touches on this book. I realized I couldn't complete a book about what the Lord was showing me if I hadn't lived the applications necessary to speak from a perspective of personal experience.

Believe me, there have been many years of living and practical application of God's truth over these last

24 years since "Step Into The Sunshine" was conceived. Possibly the longest "gestation period" for a book, but necessary. I am grateful that the Lord never removed the desire from my heart to complete this book.

I was tempted to start over from the beginning. Although my perspective and writing style have evolved, my life story hasn't changed. What was planted in my life as a child was an important part of developing me into the woman I have become. It has been because of the trials God allowed me to experience that I have been able to encourage others of God's faithfulness.

My life has been full and our family has grown since this book was originally conceived. Let me catch you up on some highlights as to what has taken place and where we are as a family in 2011.

Christina is everything a mother could possibly dream for in a daughter. She is a vision of beauty that runs deep beneath the surface, flowing through her veins to the heart that she has shared so freely with me over the years.

Christina has had to deal with her share of shade in her life. Not long after my husband's illness, while

Christina was still in High School, I began noticing behaviors that concerned me. I confronted Christina and she confessed that she had been struggling with bulimia. This was devastating as we realized the seriousness of this eating disorder. Once it was out in the open, it was as if she was relieved and could now work on getting a handle on it.

We attended a support group for eating disorders for a time. She assured me that she would seek help if it got out of hand again. She has controlled this tendency for the most part over the years. However, like so many things we invite into our lives, they will continue to knock on our door to see if they can be a part of our lives again. I would go into detail, but that is an entire book in itself!

I intend to begin assembling my notes for a book on parenting. It will include Christina and Chad contributing their insight from a child's point of view as well as today's perspective. It should be very insightful now that they each have growing families of their own.

After graduating from high school, Christina lived at home until she was married in March of 1993. While she was living with us, she was working full time and attending Boise State University. We decided to become *roommates* with Christina. It was easier to start eliminating being so instructional when we viewed her as a roommate. She was like a sponge her last couple years at home. She was open, asking for opinions as she shared her feelings and her life with us.

While in her third year at BSU, Christina met a young man that caught her eye and captured her heart. Christina was in what we referred to as the "catch and release" method of dating. She liked baiting the hook, casting the line and reeling in the catch. She seemed to lose interest once she had the catch on board. However, when Chris Gredler caught her eye, she set the hook, deciding to hang up her fishing pole for good.

Christina and Chris were married in 1993. We love Chris as he brings so much to the family. He has a wonderful sense of humor, sense of loyalty and is always up for adventure. He loves challenging himself to try something new.

Chris and Christina have been blessed with two beautiful children, John Douglas and McKenzie Wray.

John turned Doug and LaDonna into "Grandpa and Grandma" and our life has never been the same. A role we have cherished as it gives us an opportunity to love our children from a different angle.

McKenzie was our first granddaughter, joining our family five days after John's first birthday. We are blessed to live so close to Christina's family, being able to share in the different stages of their growth...many sleepovers, camping trips and holidays together and just hanging out playing games and watching movies.

On May 22, 2001, our family experienced a crisis that caused our roots to dig deeper into the very bedrock of our foundation. Words of encouragement I had spoken to others over the years were now what I was clinging to myself.

Doug and I were on the East Coast visiting Chad who was stationed at Ft. Drum, NY. We were meeting a "friend of his" for the first time and the four of us had planned to drive down the coast to North Carolina to visit my brother and his family. Dennis and his wife, Nancy, had rented a beach house for us to gather at for a few days. We were looking forward to meeting their children, Dennis and Kathleen, for the first time as well as spending quality time getting to know Chad's friend, Tracey.

The morning after we arrived, we got a phone call from our son-in-law, Chris. He told us Christina was in the hospital and was paralyzed from the waist down. She had not been in an accident nor had she fallen. She was teaching school and had been experiencing horrible back pain. When she began to lose feeling in her legs, she called Chris and he immediately took her to the emergency room.

At the time he called us in North Carolina, which was the day after she had been admitted to the hospital, they still did not know what was causing the paralysis. While she was in the examining room waiting to be seen, the paralysis moved up to mid trunk, causing her to lose the ability to sit up on her own.

I was trying to process all Chris was saying, as he was struggling with his own emotions. He had stayed strong for Christina but relating the situation to her parents created a flood of emotions he had been harboring.

I was experiencing shock, confusion, shallow breathing, and disbelief, all attacking my senses at the same time. When I hung up the phone I quickly relayed the news to my family. Everyone grabbed a phone and started calling airlines to get Doug and me back to Boise as soon as possible.

My sweet, precious, soon to be daughter-in-law, Tracey, took me down stairs and asked if she could pray for me. What a novel idea! I remember the very real sense of knowing that God was taking care of Christina. I also remember the specific thought of wondering how many lives Christina would touch with her strong faith in God. For some reason I knew that no matter what the outcome would be, that God had the final edit on her life story and that it would be for His glory. However, during this blurred period of time, I had not thought to stop and pray.

God grafted Tracey into our family that day. She walked with us through this crisis and was a great support to Chad and our entire family.

My brother located a killer deal on airline tickets, enabling us to fly out of Raleigh the next morning at

7:00 a.m. When we arrived at the hospital, the cause of the paralysis was still not known. After days of tests, ruling out Muscular Dystrophy and several other possibilities, it was determined that Christina had suffered a spinal stroke. Very unusual as several of her nurses had never cared for a patient who had suffered a spinal stroke.

After a week of testing and evaluation, Christina was transferred to Elks Rehabilitation Hospital. At this time she couldn't roll over by herself or sit up without assistance. The possibly of ever walking again was not looking feasible. The objective was to teach her the skills she would need to learn how to function from a wheelchair.

After hours of physical therapy Christina began to regain trunk control. She was then able to learn techniques of transferring herself from a bed to her wheelchair, how to move around a kitchen from wheelchair, including baking cookies. Christina knew the therapists were simply doing their job, but she assured them that she would not be doing these things from a wheelchair.

Christina's attitude was amazing and inspiring to all her visitors as well as the staff at the Elks Rehab. She always had a smile on her face and was determined she would not spend the rest of her life in a wheelchair. When people would come to visit Christina, and she had a constant stream of visitors, she would be the one cheering them up, making them comfortable in a very uncomfortable situation. She appreciated their concern but didn't want their pity. In her heart, she knew she would walk again.

Christina's favorite worship song at church was "I Walk By Faith." Needless to say, this song that captured her heart years earlier had now become an anthem that expressed her deep faith and determination. Each time this song was sung at church, Christina would motion to Chris to help her out of her wheelchair so she could stand hanging on to the chairs in front of her. She just knew that God would heal her legs and thought it would be awesome to have a little music to go with the miracle! Have I mentioned what an amazing, determined woman Christina is?

The day had finally arrived and Christina was released to go home after a month in the Hospital. She was so excited as she entered her home in a wheel chair and was greeted by her four year old son and three year old daughter. John and McKenzie were thrilled to have their mommy home with them again. She was also greeted with a fresh litter of puppies that were born while she was in the hospital!

Although Christina and her family lived in a two story home, she was determined that she was going to sleep in her own bed, which was located on the second floor. The stairs were steep but she pulled herself up, step by step, every night. Let me just say if we needed a jar of pickles opened, we would ask Christina. She had some serious, strong arms!

Christina began to get strength in her legs as she was relentless with trying to walk. Before long she graduated to a walker, then to crutches and finally to a cane. She now walks unassisted and has reached levels of recovery that none of the therapists imagined. She did receive her miracle and she still loves the song "Walk By Faith."

One of my coworkers gave me a "Footprints" flip calendar by Margaret Fishback Powers as a gift after Christina's stroke. Out of curiosity I flipped back to May 22, the day Christina had suffered the stroke. It read, "The **steps** of a good man are ordered by the Lord, as well as his **stops**." (G. Mueller) *The Lord is good to those whose hope is in Him* - Lamentations 3:25. Followed by, He whispered, *"My precious child, I love you and will never leave you."*

I still use that calendar and each year I am reminded of God's faithfulness and timing on what would have seemed to be a 'random thought on a random day' that blessed and encouraged me long before we knew the outcome of Christina's prognosis.

My faith was strengthened by watching Christina's faith grow deeper and more personal as she continued to touch so many lives with her courage and determination. She was a teacher at the time of the stroke but wasn't sure she wanted go back into the classroom. She had so much support and encouragement from fellow teachers, family and friends that she eventually made the decision to override her feelings of fear and anxiety. Her decision was confirmed when she was named "Teacher of the Year" in her school the following year.

"I can't do that" was a phrase her students knew was not allowed in her classroom. Parents requested Christina for their children because of her inspiration to all those around her. Everyone knew where her strength came from. They knew she had an awesome God whom she trusted completely.

Chris was a rock and never left her side. He encouraged her and supported her decisions to move forward. He was protective and yet did not hover. He could see her determination and wasn't going to discourage her in any way from reaching her full potential.

He encouraged her to go to a meeting about an Adaptive Ski program called Recreation Unlimited. She agreed to try skiing, finding new freedom flying down the mountain as fast as everyone else in the sit down ski equipment.

Chris has been trained to be an instructor with Recreation Unlimited and Christina is still active with the program as well currently serving on their Board.

Christina's children were three and four at the time of her stroke. At the time of this writing they are 14 and 15. They are both very compassionate young people. When McKenzie was thirteen she trained a CCI (Canine Companion Independence) puppy for fifteen months. The program was a perfect fit for her. She had first-hand experience of watching her mother in a limited capacity while she was recovering in a wheelchair as well as having a love of animals. Giga, a black lab puppy, became a temporary member of the Gredler family. Although she only spent fifteen months in their home, I know she will spend a lifetime in their hearts.

I had the opportunity to travel to California at the end of the training period with the family as McKenzie handed Giga over to the professional trainers to complete her training. It was a very emotional time for all the trainers and families involved.

The "Graduation Ceremony," when the dogs are presented to the candidates by their original trainers was very emotional. It was touching to see the joy expressed by those who had received a CCI dog as well as the sense of bittersweet farewell by those who had become so attached to the puppies they received when they were 8 weeks old.

Our grandson, John, was so moved by the experience that shortly after they returned home and with his family's blessing he applied for a puppy to raise as well. He was accepted as a trainer and has received Geralene, a Yellow Lab-Retriever mix CCI puppy to train for fifteen months. He is looking forward to being a part of providing a service dog for someone who needs assistance.

Both John and McKenzie have grown spiritually through this experience as they have watched their mother's progress over the years and seen God's plan unfold in their lives. Jeremiah 29:11...*"For I know the plans that I have for you, declares the Lord, plans for welfare and not for calamity to give you a future and a hope."*

From the time of the stroke in 2001 there has not been a night when McKenzie hasn't continued to ask God for a complete healing for her mother. For years, as a small child, McKenzie would pray, "Please God, help mommy to walk again." One evening while she was spending the night and we were saying prayers together I said to her, "Sweetheart, you do know that your mommy is walking again."

She paused and then said, "Please, God, help mommy to run again!" To this day she continues to pray the same prayer. I believe Christina's faith and persistence has been passed down to her children.

The adversity that stormed through this family in 2001 did not blow our family away but strengthened us individually as we all learned to "walk by faith."

When Chad graduated from high school, he left home and attended Treasure Valley Community College. He completed his Associates Degree while he also played College baseball.

Just as some plants are successfully growing in the pots they come in, others need transplanting in order to grow. This was true of our two children. Christina was content with staying in Boise and living with us, while Chad needed to leave home in order to grow into the man God had created him to be.

After graduating from Treasure Valley, Chad chose a military career and joined the United States Army. We could not be more proud of him. Over the years he has had the opportunity to serve on several bases in this country and around the world.

Chad was stationed in El Gora, Egypt for a year-long deployment. Doug and I were able to visit him for two weeks and had the opportunity to go on a military tour of the Holy Land. It was a blessing to spend fourteen days with Chad as we explored the places in the Bible that have now became more of a reality to all of us.

Chad met Tracey Willis while stationed in Ft. Drum, New York. She was in his Company and was serving eight years in the military. She noticed something different about Chad that caught her attention and began to capture her heart. Chad, his fellow soldier, Sean, and Tracey began hanging out together, taking in the sights up and down the East Coast.

Chad invited Tracey to attend a "Kingdom Bound" concert in upstate New York. While they were at the concert, enjoying the music from several Christian bands, Tracey went forward and accepted Jesus as her Lord and Savior. They were just friends at the time but God had bigger plans for this friendship! I do believe what originally caught her attention was his relationship with the Lord. He was also respectful, dedicated, family oriented and I might add, a mighty handsome soldier that knew how to treat a woman with respect. Just giving you my unbiased, honest opinion as a mother.

Chad is an athlete and while going to High School and College, his attention was more on sports than girls. He didn't see the need for relationships that would take his attention off his focus on soccer, basketball or baseball.

We knew when Chad began mentioning Tracey's name in our conversations when he called from Ft. Drum that she must be pretty special. Chad has always liked his own space and although he has had close buddies since grade school, he prefers a small circle of friends.

Chad and Tracey finished their service at Ft. Drum, New York and caravaned across the states, stopping along the way to take in the sites and joined our family in Montana for a cousin's wedding. Tracey had the opportunity to meet both sides of our family for the first time. She was looking forward to meeting Christina as she already felt a bond had formed over the months following her stroke.

When Christina first met Tracey, I asked her privately what she thought of this woman that had obviously caught her brother's eye. Christina said, "If she wasn't going to be my sister-in-law, she would be my best friend." They hit it off immediately and to this day they are best of friends.

Chad and Tracey were married in May of 2002. Tracey asked Christina to be a bridesmaid in their wedding. There wasn't a dry eye in the church when Chris escorted Christina down the aisle as she walked slowly to the front of the church and stood unassisted during the entire ceremony. One year from the date of the stroke and so many blessings. God is good and so faithful!

It was a beautiful wedding with Doug as Chad's best man, Chris and Christina as groomsman and bridesmaid and John and McKenzie as flower girl and ring bearer. I had a front row seat as I observed my entire family at the front of the church. Such a beautiful reflection of answered prayers, surrounded by family and friends who had loved us and supported us through this journey we were on.

Chad and Tracey were also attended by Tracey's sister, Rachel, soon to be sister-in-law Crystal, and brothers Mike and John. As well as fellow soldiers they had both served with, Heidi, Sean and Eric. We couldn't love Tracey more as she is a beautiful, loving addition to our family.

Chad joined the Idaho National Guard when he finished his six year commitment with the Army. He is a full time employee of the Guard and, having set his goals high, has been promoted to the rank of CW2.

Tracey chose to end her active Military career and, in her own words, "to be a full time girl." She and Chad bought their first home and began adding their own touches. Chad knew there would be a deployment in his future, so they chose a home near to us so Tracey would be close to family.

When rumors of deployment became a reality, we learned that Chad and Tracey were expecting their first child. We were excited to welcome a new baby into our family and were grateful that Chad would have the opportunity to be home for the birth of Kaitlynn Ann.

When Kaitlynn was three months old, Chad was deployed to Afghanistan for 16 months. It was a long deployment that caused us to grow in our faith as we completely entrusted our son's safety and that of his fellow soldiers into God's hands. My faith now moved from what I read to what I knew to be true.

Chad has a soldier's heart and a fierce loyalty to his country. On one of our phone conversations I outright asked him if he would die for this country. Without hesitation he replied, "Absolutely, in a heartbeat."

When friends would ask me if I was afraid for Chad when he went to Egypt and then to Afghanistan, I would always reply with the same sentiment. "No, I am not afraid for Chad because I know where he will be if he doesn't return home."

I had a pastor who told me that when things look ominous and perhaps frightening, to take the situation to the worse case you could imagine and work your way back. In this situation, the worst thing that could happen would be that Chad would be killed while serving his country.

It was his choice to become a soldier and ultimately his choice to die for our country. If that were to happen, then I knew he would be home with the Lord. God gave both Doug and me amazing peace while he was deployed.

Chad has been an excellent example to his soldiers of a Godly man who sets the bar high when it comes to character building and family commitment.

Chad and Tracey have been blessed with two additional children. Joshua Douglas and Allison Marita have joined their sister Kaitlynn Ann. We are fortunate to live so close to them. After having Chad gone for so many years, we are making up for lost time.

Christina and Chad have grown through their life experiences. God has stretched them and strengthened them just as He did Doug and me.

Doug and I were blessed and privileged to be asked into the delivery room with all five of our grandchildren. These babies were surrounded by so much love from the moment they were born and covered with prayer. We are blessed beyond measure and humbled with gratitude for what the Lord has done in all of our lives.

Last May I was prepared to come to McCall to finish this book. However, my dad passed away the day before I was scheduled to leave. Instead of working on the book, I spent my time writing "Reflections and Observations" of my Dad's life for his Memorial Service. As I was reflecting on my Dad's life and composing the eulogy, the memories and thoughts that began to appear on paper, continued to heal "this girl's" heart.

I facilitate a non-denominational church service at South Boise Women's Correctional Center every Sunday afternoon. I thought the women might enjoy the thoughts I had captured of how God had reconciled my heart with my Dad over the years. When I finished reading the reflections and observations of my Dad's life there were tears in several of the women's eyes. They too had experienced "father issues."

I also shared my Dad's Eulogy at a Women's Leadership Retreat. Again, several women had *father issues*...two opposite settings with women experiencing the same void in their lives.

During a quiet time at the Leadership Retreat I was praying about my Dad and began to record thoughts that were flooding my mind. It came as a letter and, even though I believe it was for me from my Heavenly Father, there is no doubt in my mind that He wanted me to share these words with others...

May 30, 2009

My Precious Daughter,

I have loved you from before you were conceived. I have known you and have placed purpose in your life. I have never taken My eyes off you nor have I prevented those things that have drawn you closer to me.

It was through the voids in your life that I filled you. It was through the frustrations that I renewed you. It was through the hurts that I established My righteousness in you.

Not one tear that has fallen from your eyes has gone unnoticed. Please remember that tears wash the windows of your soul.

As your tears have fallen, I have not forsaken you but have caught them in My hand. They have been the balm of healing that covers the scars from the pruning that is taking place in your life.

Trust Me as I have trusted you throughout the process. Trusting you to be My voice of hope to others who long for a Father's love.

It has been a deceitful plan from the beginning in the garden to distort My words and to destroy My image as a Father who could be trusted. To question My authority has weakened the authority I placed as the head of the family.

Remove the chains of bondage. Just as others removed the grave cloths from Lazarus when I called him forth from the grave, so must you, through forgiveness, release your father so that you may walk free.

Restore - refill - renew and remain in My love which is pure and don't expect your earthly father to fill the void that is for Me alone to fill. Don't wait until you understand, simply rest in knowing.

When you refuse to release your father, you hold him in the prison of your expectations. Your validation comes from Me and Me alone. Do not settle for coun-

terfeit validation. What more validation could you want than the blood that My Son shed for you?

You are loved beyond measure and perfected for My purpose. I will never leave you or forsake you. I will not deny you or deprive you. You are the apple of My eye and a sweet aroma to My nostrils.

Don't let your "history" control your destiny. I am willing to pick up anything you are willing to lay down.

Love ~ Your Father

P.S. What you don't work out, you will act out. Let it go!

This letter from the Lord has encouraged others as we are reminded that God is in control and that our biggest disappointments usually follow our highest expectations which are often unrealistic.

Doug and I have enjoyed our empty nest. We are blessed to have our children and their families living close to us. Doug is still my best friend. Through the stretching, growing and leaning into the wind, we still stand firmly committed to one another. We've learned the depths of a long-term commitment, and recognize when the enemy has been allowed to kick up his heels. We have seen God's grace in mended hearts and emotions. We have truly learned the meaning of love.

We have seen God's love through the laughter of our children and grandchildren and through the hardest of times. We have experienced a wonderful buffet of life, and have tasted many of its selections. For some I would go back for seconds, for some I would rather not, but I am thankful to have had a taste. Psalms 34:8 tells us to, *"Taste and see that the Lord is good."*

We have experienced a harvest from our home, as I know many of you have. A harvest is to be shared and celebrated.

Everyone who has ever lived in Boise knows that the least favorite month is February. The ever-present inversion leaves our city in a state of gloom for several weeks. As I was driving across town in February, the sun pierced the sky, and the inversion began to lift like a blanket. Even the newscasters were commenting on how everyone's spirits seemed to lift with the arrival of the sunshine. For days, people were almost silly as they celebrated the sun.

It occurred to me that February in Boise is what our lives would be without Christ. He is the Son, and the Light of the World. Without Him, we are left in a darkness that is void of light.

Thank you for taking this time to "Step Into The Sunshine" with me, and for allowing me to share my heart with you. I pray that you will look for and find joy in your journey and be that *ray of sunshine everywhere you go, shining for your Master with a steady glow*! Let His Light illuminate your path as you discover all that God has for you!

Points to Ponder...

What harvest have you anticipated over the years?

How have you seen God move through this season of your life?

The night before I came to McCall, I felt like a race horse eager to get out of the gate and onto the track. I couldn't wait to start putting my thoughts down on paper after so many years of observing, taking notes and praying. I was ready to take the first steps to push this book closer to a reality.

Have you ever had a dream that is identical each time? Suddenly the dream that I had repeatedly experienced for years was beginning to make sense. In this particular dream, I am suddenly naked in the middle of crowds of people. I would be walking down the street naked. Total exposure! It occurred to me that this was the position I could be putting myself in by beginning to write this book. It might be easier to walk down the street naked than to reveal my inner thoughts, exposing them to ridicule and criticism! I knew it was risky but I was ready to begin. (Just a random thought I wanted to share.)

CPSIA information can be obtained at www.ICGtesting.com
Printed in the USA
BVOW061635120312

284897BV00002B/1/P